CHARLES B. RAMSKOV
CHARLES B. RAMSKOV
CHARLES B. RAMSKOV
CHARLES B. RAMSKOV

PSYCHOLOGY NOTES

SECOND EDITION

De Anza College

Kendall Hunt
publishing company

Image credits:

Pages 14, 28, and 55 line drawings by Devin Ramskov

Pages 11, 29-31—Images copyright Kendall Hunt Publishing Company

Cover image © Shutterstock, Inc.

www.kendallhunt.com
Send all inquiries to:
4050 Westmark Drive
Dubuque, IA 52004-1840

Copyright © 2008, 2013 by Charles B. Ramskov

ISBN: 978-1-4652-3206-9

Printed in the United States of America

10 9 8 7 6 5 4 3 2 1

ACKNOWLEDGMENTS

I would sincerely like to thank Professor Frank Savage for all he has done for the De Anza Psychology Department and for the foundational help provided for this work and for his mentoring. I would also like to thank Professor Linda M. Hurkmans for her tireless efforts on this project. Thank you to my son, Devin Ramskov, for his help on the illustrations.

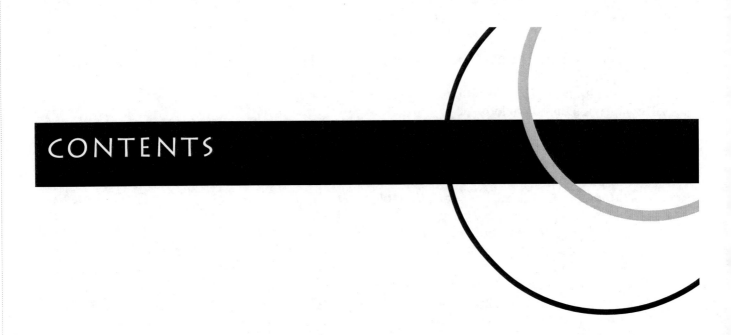

CONTENTS

CHAPTER 2

BRAIN STRUCTURE AND FUNCTION   9

CHAPTER 3

LIFE-SPAN DEVELOPMENT 15

CHAPTER 4

CONSCIOUSNESS—SLEEP, DREAMS, AND DRUGS 21

CHAPTER 5
SENSATION   27

CHAPTER 6
PERCEPTION   33

CHAPTER 7
LEARNING: BASIC PROCESSES   37

CHAPTER 1

The Scope and Goals of Psychology

I. A Definition of Psychology

A. What Is Psychology?

According to one popular definition of psychology, psychology is "The science that studies behavior and its underlying physiological and cognitive processes."

PSYCHOLOGY AS A BEHAVIORAL SCIENCE:
Psychology is related to biology, genetics, neuroscience, physiology, chemistry, physics, and computer science.

PSYCHOLOGY AS A SOCIAL SCIENCE:
Psychology is related to sociology, anthropology, economics, and political science and law.

PSYCHOLOGY AS A CLINICAL SCIENCE:
Psychology is a clinically applied discipline that addresses treatment and research relating to mental disorders and mental health.

PSYCHOLOGY AS A COGNITIVE SCIENCE:
Psychology as a cognitive science reflects the contemporary focus on cognitive processes involved in perception, memory language, imagery, problem solving, and decision making.

B. Goals and Themes of Psychology

Goals:

1. Description
2. Explanation
3. Prediction/Control
4. Improve Life

Major Themes:

1. Empiricism
2. Theoretical Diversity
3. Sociohistorical Context
4. Multiple Causation
5. Heredity and Environment

II. Philosophical and Scientific Background of Psychology

A. Early Greeks

Twenty-five hundred years ago the early Greeks asked many of the same questions psychologists are concerned with today.

<u>What</u> is knowledge? What does it mean when we say we "know" something?

<u>How</u> is knowledge acquired and stored?

How do the processes of perception, learning, and memory relate to knowledge acquisition?

Hippocrates (460-377 B.C.) Hippocrates was the father of medicine who believed that disease was not a punishment sent by the gods but was due to natural causes. Hippocrates used **empirical** observations to study medical issues and employed dissection and vivisection to study both human and animal anatomy and physiology based on the belief that he could generalize from animals to humans.

HIPPOCRATES thought that the mind (or "soul") and body were qualitatively different **(mind-body dualism).** Hippocrates also formulated the theory of bodily **humors—blood, black bile, yellow bile, and phlegm.** He developed a theory of **four temperaments** based on the four humors.

SOCRATES (469-399 B.C.) Important quotations: "Know thyself." "The unexamined life is not worth living."

PLATO (427-347 B.C.) Plato believed that knowledge is **inborn** or **innate (Nativism).** And like Socrates, Plato was a **Rationalist** who thought that sensations are imperfect representations of reality, as illustrated in the **Allegory of the Cave.** "Knowledge does not derive from sensations but from <u>reasoning about</u> sensations." Plato stressed the difference between sensations and **"Forms or Ideas,"** which Plato saw as eternal universal structures or pure abstract ideas exemplified in mathematical principles and natural laws. Plato thought that the psyche and the body were different entities (Dualism), but the mind and the body influenced each other (Interactionistic Dualism).

ARISTOTLE (385-322 B.C.) Aristotle was an **Empiricist** who believed that the mind at birth is a blank tablet or **(tabula rasa)** and we acquire knowledge through **experience** and **observation.** He used the **inductive** approach that derives general principles from many careful observations of specific phenomena rather than Plato's **deductive** approach that uses reason and logic to deduce general principles. **Aristotle also formulated three "laws" of associative memory; similarity, contrast,** and **contiguity** are reflected in contemporary studies of memory and learning.

B. The Late Renaissance (1300s to 1600s) and the Birth of Science

RENE DESCARTES (1596-1650) Descartes agreed with **Plato's mind-body-dualism** by hypothesizing that the body was entirely material and operated in a purely mechanical way because muscle movements and the circulation of the blood are machine-like. The rational mind or "soul" was viewed as non-material, spiritual and unextended, i.e., does not exist in space or time. Descartes also agreed with **Plato's rationalism** and **innate** knowledge.

Descartes's belief in the **interaction of mind and body** prompted him to speculate that the connection between mind and body occurred at a centrally located and unduplicated brain structure called the **pineal gland.** He thought that soul or "animal spirits" **interacted** with the body through the pineal gland. He proposed that the images from each retina were fused together at the pineal gland to project a single focused image representing eternal reality. In addition, he thought that all muscle movement originated at the pineal gland by sending the "animal spirits" down the hollow nerves to the muscles. According to Descartes, there is a two-way interaction between the mind and body, but the body is subordinate to the mind.

Descartes's search for certainty lead him to develop a method of systematic doubt. What could he be certain of without any possibility of doubt? His answer was that that he could not doubt that he was doubting (i.e., thinking), which in turn meant that he existed. Descartes's famous statement **"Cogito ergo sum,"** "I think, therefore I am," captures the central idea that the certainty of his thinking and, therefore of his existence could not be doubted.

C. British Empiricism (1600s to 1800s)

THOMAS HOBBES (1588-1679) rejected Descartes's **interactionistic dualism,** in which the mind and body are viewed as separate entities that interact. Instead, Hobbes held a view called **materialistic monism,** wherein the mind and body (brain) both consist of a **single material** substance. Hobbes conceived of sensation, thinking, and consciousness as being due to the motion of atoms in the brain. He was also the first to reject Descartes's notion of **innate ideas** and held that the content of the mind comes only from **sensory experience** and not from innate ideas. Hobbes considered human nature to be basically aggressive and selfish. According to Hobbes, "Without government the life of man is solitary, selfish, poor, nasty, brutish, and short."

JOHN LOCKE (1632-1704) rejected also the doctrine of innate ideas espoused by Descartes and Plato and asserted that **all ideas come from experience.** The mind is a blank slate or **tabula rasa** at birth, capable only of passively receiving stimuli from the environment and reflecting on these sensory experiences.

D. Rationalism and Empiricism Integrated

EMMANUAL KANT (1724-1804) Rationalism and empiricism were integrated by Kant who proposed that knowledge comes from sensory perception; this perception is not of things as they really are, but only as they appear to us (phenomena); and we perceive phenomena according to the nature of preexisting forms or **a priori categories.** Kant called these categories "activities of the mind" that consist of intuitive and universal givens. The Kantian categories of unity, time, space, and causality provide the potential basis for structuring and ordering our sensory experience into an organized and unitary world of objects within a meaningful context. The mind is not simply a passive recipient of sensory information but rather it is seen as an active organizing agent. We perceive phenomena the way our mind presupposes us to see them.

III. Historical Survey of Psychology as a Science

A. The Founding Fathers

1. **Willhelm Wundt (1832–1920)**
   a. Founded the first experimental psychology laboratory in Germany's University of Leipzig in 1879
   b. The Structural School was founded and developed by Wundt. Defined as the attempt to analyze the consciousness into fundamental elements, including sensations, images, and feelings.
   c. The structure of the mind was viewed as a combination of mental elements.
   d. Introspection was the method used by structuralists to analyze conscious experience.

Wilhelm Wundt.

2. **William James (1842–1910)**
   a. Stream of consciousness and a theory of emotion based on feedback from bodily processes
   b. Associated units
   c. The Functional School of Psychology emphasized adjustment and adaptation to the environment rather than the structure of consciousness and reflected Darwin's theory of natural selection and the pragmatism of John Dewey.
   d. Wrote *The Principles of Psychology* (1890)
   e. Interests of early psychologists, as James defined them, were people's feelings, desires, thoughts, reasoning, and decisions—as well as their struggles to attain their goals or to become reconciled to failure.
3. **Edward B. Tichner (1867-1927)**
   a. British Psychologist studied under Wundt created his version of Structuralism
   b. Created the largest Doctoral program in Psychology at Cornell University
   c. His first graduate student was also first women to receive a PhD in Psychology in 1894
4. **G. Stanley Hall (1844-1924)**
   a. American Psychologist and Educator was an American Structuralist
   b. Earned his doctorate in Psychology under William James at Harvard
   c. First American doctorate in Psychology worked in Wundt's lab in 1879
   d. First president of the American Psychological Association
   e. Founded the American Journal of Psychology, Brought Freud and Jung to the U.S.

    5. **Francis Gallon (1880s)**
       a. Measurement of individual differences
       b. Interest in the influence of heredity
       c. Contributed to the development of modern statistics

B. The Behaviorist Revolution

    1. **John B. Watson (1870–1958)**
       a. Father of **Behaviorism,** a focus on directly observable behavior
       b. Emphasis on movement and glandular functions ("If it doesn't twitch or squirt, it's not behavior.")
       c. Basic unit of learning was the conditioned reflex, borrowed from Pavlov's earlier work.
       d. Everything is determined by past experience. Strong emphasis on environmentalism and rejection of instinct and heredity.
    2. **B. F. Skinner (1906–1990)**
       a. Stimulus-Response (S/R) Psychology
       b. Emphasis on environmental control of behavior
       c. All behavior and learning is determined by their outcome and consequences of response determining behavior.
       d. Emphasis on description and direct observation

C. Gestalt Psychology

    1. **Max Wertheimer (1890–1943) Kurt Koffka, Wolfgang Kohler, and Kurt Lewin (c. 1920s)**
       a. Originated in Germany at the same time that Watson's behaviorism was becoming influential in the U.S.
    2. Gestalt school believes that in studying any psychological phenomena it is essential to look at the pattern considered as a whole. ("The whole is greater than the sum of its parts.")
    3. Initiated Study of Visual Perception

D. Cognitive Psychology

    1. **E. C. Tolman** Bridge between classical behaviorism and cognitive revolution of the 1960s
       a. Emphasis on higher mental processes, thinking, problem solving, decision making, perception, and "cognitive maps" or internal mental representations of the environment
       b. "Cognitive revolution" of 1960s. Inspired by the work of Piaget, Miller, Neiser, Gallaner, Pribram, Newell, and Simon. The computer is both a model of cognitive processes and a means of studying these processes through simulations and experiments.

E. Humanistic Psychology

    1. **Emphasis on the uniqueness and positive growth potential of the individual**
       a. Abraham Maslow—Self-Actualization
       b. Carl Rogers—Client-Centered Therapy
       c. Rollo May, Gordon Allport
       d. The Human Potential Movement
       e. Influenced by Existential Philosophy

F. Psychoanalysis

1. **Sigmund Freud**
   a. Unconscious processes and Psychic Determinism
   b. Developed the first method of psychotherapy—origins of Clinical Psychology
   c. Emphasis on early childhood experiences
   d. The pervasive influence of sexual drives on behavior

IV. The Methods of Psychology

Because human behavior and mental processes take such a wide variety of forms, psychologists have had to adopt a number of different ways of studying their subject matter.

A. Characteristics of Scientific Explanations

1. Scientific explanations are **EMPIRICAL**. They are based on objective, systematic observations.
2. Scientific explanations are **RATIONAL**. They follow the rules of logic and are consistent with known facts.
3. Scientific explanations are **TESTABLE**. They are verifiable through observation and can be disproved.
4. Scientific explanations are **PARSIMONIOUS**. They provide the simplest explanation using the fewest possible assumptions.
5. Scientific explanations are **GENERAL**. They apply beyond the original observations on which they are based.
6. Scientific explanations are **TENTATIVE**. They are never accepted as absolutely correct.
7. Scientific explanations are **RIGOROUSLY EVALUATED**. They are constantly evaluated for consistency with evidence, generality, and parsimony.

Major Figures in the Formation and Development of Six Psychological Systems										
1870	1880	1890	1900	1910	1920	1930	1940	1950	1960	
STRUCTURALISM										
	Wundt		Titchener		Hall					
		FUNCTIONALISM								
	James		Dewey	Angell		Carr	McGeoch		Melton	
						Woodworth			Underwood	
	ASSOCIATIONISM									
	Ebbinghaus			Pavlov		Bekhterev	Thorndike	Guthrie		Estes
					BEHAVIORISM					
					Watson	Hunter	Skinner		Spence	
			Meyer		Welss		Tolman	Hull Miller		
					GESTALT THEORY					
					Wertheimer	Köhler				
Mach	von Ehrenfels				Kollka					
	PSYCHOANALYSIS									
	Breuer Freud		Adler Rank Jones				Horney	Sullivan		Fromm
			Jung Ferenczi							

Source: The Book of Psyche, 2007.

B. The Scientific Method: Four Steps

1. **Observing a Phenomenon**
   Through observation of a phenomenon, you identify the **VARIABLES** that appear to be important in explaining behavior.
2. **Formulating Tentative Explanations**
   Initial observations lead to the development of a **HYPOTHESIS,** or tentative statement, about the relationship among the variables identified.
3. **Further Observing and Experimenting**
   You carry out more detailed **OBSERVATIONS** of the behavior of interest. These observations are directed at testing your hypothesis.
4. **Refining and Retesting Explanations**
   Supported hypotheses are often **REFINED** and subjected to further exploration. Disconfirmed hypotheses may be reworked and **RETESTED.**

C. The Experiment

1. **Independent and Dependent Variables**
   a. Independent—variables that the experimenter directly controls and manipulates, usually a stimulus
   b. Dependent—response or change in the behavior produced by the independent variable-concomitant variation
   c. Intervening—variables not directly observable; inferred inner states that "explain the relationship between the independent and dependent variables. Such concepts as "drive" and intelligence are intervening variables.
   d. Operational definitions of variables—(What do you mean?) operations or manipulations that define a concept
2. **The Control Group**
   Methods of controlling extraneous variables other than the independent variable that may affect the experimental outcome include holding variables constant across or randomizing their effects across conditions.
   a. Random sampling—representative samples
   b. Random assignment of subjects to experimental and control group conditions
   c. Matching subjects on relevant variables: between-groups design
   d. Using the subject as his/her own control: within group design
   e. Placebos as a control for expectation and suggestion
   f. The need to establish baseline performance to provide a basis for comparison between the before treatment and after treatment conditions
   g. The functional relationship between values or levels of the independent variable and the dependent variable; some relationships are monotonic, others are curvilinear—observed effects on the dependent variable depend on the level of the independent variable.
3. **Single Blind and Double Blind**
   a. Single Blind—Subjects have no knowledge of control assignment.
   b. Double Blind—Both subject and experimenter have no knowledge of control assignment.
4. **The Advantages and Disadvantages of the Experiment**
   a. To replicate other experiments in order to verify their findings
   b. Greater control over relevant variables
   c. Cause and effect relationships more clearly identified
   d. Artificiality and "demand characteristics" of the experiment
   e. Confirmation bias in paradigm view
   f. Reduction methods logical flaw

D. Observation

1. **Participant**
2. **Naturalistic**
   a. Values
   b. Limitations

E. Tests—Both Psychological and Physiological

Ability, attitude, feelings, motives, opinion, intelligence, and personality

F. Interviews and Case Histories, Archival Research

G. Questionnaires/Surveys

Major method for gathering information from large numbers of subjects

H. Correlational Methods

Psychometrics and individual differences

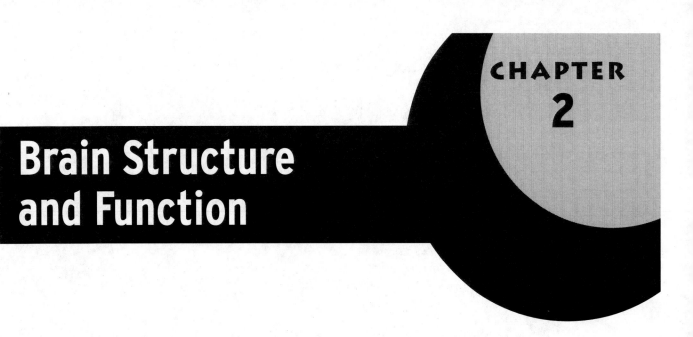

Brain Structure and Function

CHAPTER 2

I. Gross Brain Anatomy

A. Hemispheres and Lobes

1. **Left and right hemispheres**—separated by the medial longitudinal fissure and connected by the corpus callosum
2. **Frontal lobes**—muscle movement and speech (Broca's speech area)
3. **Parietal lobes**—skin and muscle senses
4. **Temporal lobes**—hearing, speech (Wernicke's speech area)
5. **Occipital lobes**—vision

B. Significant Terms

1. **Fissures**—a cleft, deep enough to indent the ventricles
2. **Sulci**—(singularsulcus) a cleft, shallower than a fissure
3. **Gyri**—(singulargyrus) a ridge
4. **Cranial**—pertaining to the head
5. **Rostral**—head or front, "beak, mouth" front
6. **Caudal**—tail or hind end
7. **Superior**—top
8. **Inferior**—lower
9. **Anterior**—front
10. **Posterior**—back of brain
11. **Dorsal**—back of the animal
12. **Ventral**—belly or front/anterior
13. **Ipsilateral**—same side
14. **Contralateral**—opposite sides
15. **Medial**—midline or center
16. **Lateral**—side
17. **Convolutions**—folded uneven complex (e.g., surface of the cortex)

C. Major Subdivisions of the Central Nervous System

1. **Brainstem**
   a. Diencephalon—consists of three thalamic structures
      1) Epithalamus—pineal body—circadian rhythms
      2) Thalamus
         a) Lateral geniculate nucleus (LGN)—visual system, retinal representation
         b) Medial geniculate nucleus (MGN)—auditory system relay
      3) Hypothalamus—eating, sex, sleep, temp. control, emotional reactions

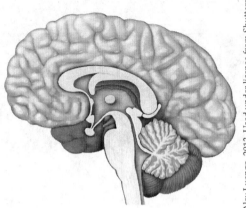

   b. Midbrain—mesencephalon
      1) Tectum
         a) Superior colliculus (anterior pair)—visual tracking and attention
         b) Inferior colliculus (posterior pair)—auditory system relay
         c) Substantia nigra (dark area)—source of dopamine
      2) Tegmentum—dorsal part of the midbrain
   c. Hindbrain
      1) Cerebellum
      2) Pons
      3) Reticular formation
      4) Medulla oblongata
2. **Forebrain**
   a. Neocortex—six-layered structure overlying the archicortex on top of the thalamus
   b. Limbic system—includes the hypothalamus, amygdala, septal area, and hippocampus which carry messages between higher and lower parts of the brain. It plays important roles in controlling the visceral organs, in emotion and memory, and in adaptive behavior.
   c. Basal ganglia—a group of large nuclei in the forebrain that are related to changes in posture, increases or decreases in muscle tone, and abnormal movements such as twitches, jerks, and tremors
   d. Thalamus—the relay station connecting the lower structures of the brain and the spinal cord with the cerebrum
   e. Olfactory Bulbs and Tract
3. **Spinal Cord**—(reflex arc)
   a. Dorsal tracts (posterior in humans)—sensory
   b. Ventral tracts (anterior in humans)—motor
4. **Autonomic Nervous System**
   a. Sympathetic nervous system
   b. Parasympathetic nervous system

II. Neurons: Structure

A. Neuron

A cell specialized to receive, process, and/or transmit information to other cells within the body, 3 basic parts: dendrite, cell body, axon

1. **Dendrites**—extensions of the cell body which receive "information" in the form of chemical neurotransmitters or electrical events from other cells

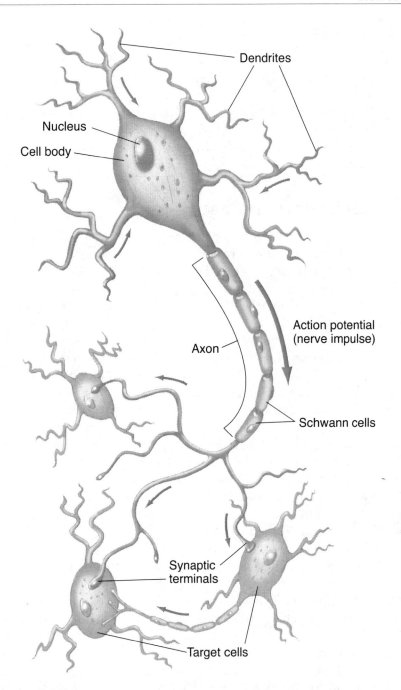

2. **Cell Body (Soma)**—the area of cytoplasm that surrounds the nucleus
   a. Nucleus—a spherical structure in the soma of cells that contains DNA
      1) Chromosomes—deoxyribonucleic acid (DNA)
      2) Nucleolus—produces ribonucleic acid (RNA)
   b. Mitochondria Endoplasmic Reticulum (EK)
3. **Axon**—transmits information along its length to other cells (conducts)
   a. Axon hillock—initial portion of axon where it leaves the cell body, point at which the action potential is initiated
   b. Terminal buttons—the end of an axon that contains vesicles or packages of chemicals, called neurotransmitters, that, when released, influence the activity of other cells
4. **Synapse**—point of interaction between nerve cells, includes the presynaptic neuron, synaptic cleft, and the postsynaptic membrane (a more complete description to follow)
   a. Presynaptic—refers to sending neuron and its processes
   b. Postsynaptic—receiving surface of a second cell (usually a neuron)
   c. Synaptic cleft—tiny gap between presynaptic terminal and postsynaptic membrane

B. Major Types of Neurons

1. **Motor Neurons** (efferent neurons)—carry messages out away from central nervous system to muscles and glands (Bell-Magendie Law, c. 1811). Exit through ventral roots of the spinal cord
2. **Sensory Neurons** (afferent neurons)—carry messages in, toward the central nervous system. Enter through dorsal roots of the spinal cord.
3. **Interneurons**—make up 97% of all nerve cells in the human brain and are located within the CNS (central nervous system). Located between sensory and motor neurons.

C. How the Neuron Works: Charges and Ions

1. Two **characteristics of neurons** are crucial to their functioning:
   a. Concentration gradient—difference in ion concentration inside and outside the cell. Ions will diffuse from a region of high to low concentration.
   b. Electrostatic gradient—difference in electrical potential across the membrane
2. **Resting Potential**—the relatively constant charge across a neural membrane
   K+ ions at resting potential are concentrated inside, Na+ ions Outside
   Note: When a reference electrode is placed outside the nerve cell and a second electrode is placed inside the nerve cell, there is a measured membrane potential of –70 millivolts.
3. **Nerve Impulse**—movement of the action potential along the length of an axon; begins at the axon hillock. Rate of firing—generally fewer than 100 times a second, but can fire as frequently as 1000 times a second.
4. **Action Potential**—the brief electrical impulse by which information is conducted along an axon, resulting from brief changes in the membrane's permeability to potassium and sodium ions (Absolute and relative refractory periods)
5. **All-or-None Law**—When the neuron reaches its threshold (approx. –50mv.), it fires with all of its energy, in one direction and without decreasing speed. Much like the firing of a gun or the lighting of a fuse.
6. **Factors Determining Nerve Impulse Speed**
   a. Size (diameter)—larger conducts faster.
   b. Myelin—the fatty insulation around an axon; speeds firing.
   c. Nodes of Ranvier—gaps in the myelin sheath at periodic intervals, where the impulse is generated
   d. Saltatory conduction—propagation of a nerve impulse on a myelinated axon; characterized by its leaping from one node of Ranvier to another node
7. **Sodium-Potassium Pump**—Pumps 3 Na" ions back out of cell for every 2 K" ions back into the cell. The net result of this action is the restoration/maintenance of the –70mv resting potential. Na⁴ and K"¹' ions have their own channels. A typical small neuron may have as many as one million molecular pumps.
8. **Graded Potentials**—Dendritic voltage changes from the resting potential, in proportion to intensity of stimulation.
9. **Spatial and Temporal Summation**
   a. Spatial Summation—summation in which the effects of many synaptic inputs over the surface of a cell are added together
   b. Temporal Summation—summation in which the effects of synaptic inputs spaces closely in time are added together
10. **Passive Properties of Neurons**
    a. Depolarization—due to increased inward movement of Na+ ions
    b. Hyperpolarization—due to increased outward movement of K+ ions or increased or increased inward CL– movement

D. Synaptic Transmission

1. Axonal transport of enzymes and precursors needed for synthesis of transmitter agents, vesicle wall, and so forth
2. Propagation of action potential over presynaptic membrane
3. Synthesis of transmitter and its storage in vesicles
4. Depolarization of presynaptic terminal causes influx of Calcium (Ca+), which leads vesicles to fuse with release sites and to liberate transmitter into synaptic cleft.
5. Binding of transmitter to receptor molecules in postsynaptic membrane, initiating post-synaptic potential
6. Binding of transmitter to an autoreceptor in the bouton membrane
7. Enzyme present in extracellular space and in glia splits excess transmitter and prevents it from passing beyond the synaptic cleft.
8. Reuptake of transmitter stops synaptic action and provides transmitter for subsequent transmission.
9. Second messenger is released into postsynaptic neuron by certain transmitter-receptor combinations.
10. Inactivation of second messenger by enzyme
11. Postsynaptic potentials spread passively over dendrites and cell body to the axon hillock.
12. Ion channels—structure and function

E. Sites of Drug Action on Synapses

1. **Synthesis**—Precursor chemicals are synthesized in the cell body.
2. **Storage**—Synaptic vesicles receive the synthesized NT.
3. **Release**—When nerve discharges, vesicles release content into synaptic space.
4. **Receptor Interaction**—Released NT crosses the synaptic space and binds to specialized receptors on the postsynaptic membrane (Lock and Key).
5. **Inactivation**—In some synapses the NT is inactivated in the synaptic space.
6. **Reuptake**—In other synapses the NT is taken back up into the presynaptic neuron. In some synapses, both inactivation and reuptake may occur.
7. **Degradation**—Enzymatic breakdown of NT

Terminals contain a large number of Ca^{++} channels. Action Potential opens these, so that Ca^{++} ions enter the terminal. It is their entry that facilitates the release of the neurotransmitter by the synaptic vesicles into the synaptic cleft or gap.

III. Origins of the Human Brain and Behavior

A. The Evolutionary Record—Three Major Advances in the Study of Human Evolution

1. Proliferation of hominid (hominidae) fossil discoveries, allowing for morphological reconstruction. New methods that add biochemical information to morphological descriptions.
2. Protein comparisons, DNA strand comparisons (mitochondria, other)
3. New methods of behavioral analysis are beginning to disclose the evolutionary forces that sculpted modern humans. These studies are directed at humans, their proximate relatives (chimpanzees, gorillas, orangutans, and gibbons), and their more distant relatives (baboons and monkeys). (Goodall)
4. DNA-mapping—Demonstrates degree of interspecies relatedness

B. Episodic Evolution of Humankind (Punctuated Equilibrium)

Darwin believed that evolution was gradual, largely being shaped by processes of natural selection and sexual selection (fitness). As in Darwin's time there is no evidence for gradual change producing new species. Rather, speciation occurs very rapidly, probably in a few hundred or a few thousand years. The view that evolution occurs very rapidly, adopted in the 1980s, marks a major shift in evolutionary biology. The sudden appearance of new forms without evidence of transitional types is characteristic of humanoids and most other species. Sociology follows Darwin's work and became popular in 1975 with the book by E.O. Wilson: Sociobiology: The New Synthesis. The field of Evolutionary Psychology was later founded with the intent of applying evolutionary principles to the problems of human social function and behavior.

C. Brain Evolution—One Common Method of Investigation is Cranial Capacity.

1. **Cranial Capacity**—gives a reasonable estimate of brain size. Must be wary of assuming that brain size is an index of intelligence. Although human brains average 1300 cc, they range from 1000 cc to 2000 cc, with an unreliable correlation between size and apparent intelligence. This range indicates that modern brain size overlaps all but our most ancient predecessors. Neural organization is probably far more important than the mere number. Last, brain size is based on body size. The larger a body, the more neurons required to convey sensations and move muscles.

D. Neoteny

A concept that provides an explanatory mechanism that seeks to explain the evolution of humanoid brain development. In general, neoteny is related to a kind of "fixated" or arrested development that reflects the slower rate of development characteristic of the juvenile period. The juvenile gorilla and/or chimpanzee has the following features: small face, vaulted cranium, a lighter jaw structure, and attendant lighter muscular attachments. These juvenile features are seen to have provided the basis for the evolution of the large cranial capacity of Homo sapiens.

E. Neuroanatomical Comparisons

There are persuasive similarities between the brains of humans and primates.
1. **Brain Size**
   a. Brain size varies with body size.
   b. Encenphalization Quotient (EQ)—the ratio of actual brain size to expected brain size, based on an average for living mammals that takes body size into account. The average, or typical, mammal has an EQ of 1.0. Human = 6.3.
2. **Brain Structure**—Are the brains of humans significantly different from primate brains, or just larger?
   a. Total neocortex—progression index: the ratio of actual neocortex to the expected neocortex of a typical mammal

Life-Span Development

I. Introduction and Overview

A. Definitions of Development

B. Quantitative and Qualitative Changes over Time

C. Age Related Changes in Life-Span Development

1. **Prenatal** (Conception—Birth)
2. **Infancy** (Birth—2 years old)
3. **Early Childhood** (2–6 years old)
4. **Middle and Late Childhood** (6–11 years old)
5. **Adolescence** (11–18 years old)
6. **Early Adulthood** (18–40 years old)
7. **Middle Adulthood** (40–70 years old)
8. **Late Adulthood** (70—Death)

II. Methods of Studying Development

A. Baby Biographies

B. Experimental Methods

C. Correlational Approaches

D. Interview Methods

E. Longitudinal and Cross-Sectional Methods

F. Sequential

G. Archival Research

III. Areas or Stands of Development

A. Physical

B. Cognitive

C. Emotional

D. Social

E. Personality

IV. Theories and Perspectives

A. Stage Theories
    1. **Psychodynamic Perspective**
      a. Freudian Model
        1) Psychic structures and systems of personality
          a) Id
          b) Ego
          c) Superego

        2) Psychosexual stages
           a) Oral—birth to 2 years
           b) Anal—2 to 3 years
           c) Phallic—3 to 5 years
           d) Latency—5 to 12 years
           e) Genital—12 years and up
    b. Jungian Model
        1) Major concepts and structures of personality
        2) Time perspective constructs (stages)—presexual, prepubertal, youth, midlife, and old age
    c. Erik Erikson—Eight stages of psychosocial development
        1) Trust vs. mistrust (0–1 year)
        2) Autonomy vs. self-doubt (1–3 years)
        3) Initiative vs. guilt (3–6 years)
        4) Competence (industry) vs. inferiority (6–12 years)
        5) Identity vs. role confusion (12–20 years)
        6) Intimacy vs. isolation (20–40 years)
        7) Generativity vs. stagnation (40–65 years)
        8) Ego-integrity vs. despair (65 and older)
  2. **Piaget's Cognitive-Structural Perspective**
    a. Sensorimotor period (birth—2 years)
    b. Preoperational (2–7 years)
    c. Concrete Operational (7–11 years)
    d. Formal Operational (11—Adult)
  3. **Piagetian Concepts and Principles**
    a. Assimilation and accommodation
    b. Schemas and equilibrium

V. Heredity

A. Chromosomes

  1. **Cross Structure and Number**—46, 23 pairs
  2. **Human Karyotype**
  3. **Autosomes**
  4. **Sex Chromosomes**
    a. XX = Female
    b. XY = Male
  5. **Chromosomal Abnormalities**

B. Genes and DNA

  1. **DNA**—deoxyribonucleic acid
  2. **DNA Structure and Chemical Composition**—the double helix made up of:
    a. Deoxyribose sugar and phosphate backbone structure
    b. Four bases arranged in complementary base pairs
        1) Adenine—Thymine; Guanine—Cytosine
        2) These base pairs are *always* connected in the same way to the sugar-phosphate backbone of the helix by hydrogen bonds.
    c. DNA replication
    d. DNA transcription through RNA
    e. Protein synthesis through RNA and the 20 amino acids
    f. Recombinant DNA—gene splicing

C. Genetic Transcription

1. **Genotype and Phenotype**
2. **Mendel's Laws**
   a. First Law: Law of segregation
   b. Second Law: Genes on different chromosomes
   c. Alleles are alternative forms of a gene.
   d. *Homozygous* and *heterozygous* genotypes
   e. Dominant and recessive genes
   f. Dominant and recessive autosomal genes, x-linked and y-linked genes
3. **Polygenic Determination**
4. **Harmful Genes and Genetic Counseling**—PKU and Down's syndrome, etc.

D. Heredity–Environment Interaction

1. **Methods of Determining Heredity Influence**
   a. Consanguinity and pedigree studies
   b. Correlational methods
   c. Experimental and selective breeding
2. **Genetic Influences on Development**

VI. Prenatal Development Phases

A. Gametes and Fertilization

1. Meiosis Spermatogenesis and Cogenesis

B. Fertilization

C. Germinal Stage (fertilization to two weeks)

D. Embryonic Stage (two to eight weeks)

E. Fetal Stage (eight weeks to birth)

F. Environmental Influences on Prenatal Development

1. **Diet, Drugs, and Emotional Factors**
2. **Blood Type and Maternal Illnesses**
3. **Birth Defects**

G. Birth

1. **The Birth Process and Methods of Childbirth**
   a. Cesarean and medicated childbirths
   b. Grantly Dick–Read
   c. Le Boyer
   d. Lamaze
   e. Birth trauma
   f. Bonding

D. Neoteny

A concept that provides an explanatory mechanism that seeks to explain the evolution of humanoid brain development. In general, neoteny is related to a kind of "fixated" or arrested development that reflects the slower rate of development characteristic of the juvenile period. The juvenile gorilla and/or chimpanzee has the following features: small face, vaulted cranium, a lighter jaw structure, and attendant lighter muscular attachments. These juvenile features are seen to have provided the basis for the evolution of the large cranial capacity of Homo sapiens.

E. Neuroanatomical Comparisons

There are persuasive similarities between the brains of humans and primates.
1. **Brain Size**
   a. Brain size varies with body size.
   b. Encenphalization Quotient (EQ)—the ratio of actual brain size to expected brain size, based on an average for living mammals that takes body size into account. The average, or typical, mammal has an EQ of 1.0. Human = 6.3.
2. **Brain Structure**—Are the brains of humans significantly different from primate brains, or just larger?
   a. Total neocortex—progression index: the ratio of actual neocortex to the expected neocortex of a typical mammal

Consciousness–Sleep, Dreams, Drugs, and Hypnosis

I. Sleep

A. Circadian Rhythms (24 hour cycles)

24–25 hour and 90 minute activity rest cycles

B. Sleep Stages

1. **Transitional,** 5–10 minute duration, slowed breathing and heart rate, lightest level of sleep, EEG irregular, low voltage, alpha rhythms (8–12 Hz), beginning theta rhythms (5–7 Hz)
2. **Sleep Spindles** (14–18 Hz) and K complexes (large amplitude negative-positive deflections)
3. **Delta Rhythms** (.5–5 Hz) 20% of EEG
4. **Delta Rhythms,** 50% of EEG
5. **REM Sleep** (rapid eye movement)
   a. Paradoxical sleep—EEG like that of an alert person while muscles deeply relaxed
   b. EEG pattern—low voltage, high frequency, beta rhythms (above 18 Hz)
   c. Presence of dreams most frequent
   d. REM periods increase from 10 to 60 minutes throughout the night
   e. The amount of REM decreases over the lifespan.

C. Sleep Cycles

1. Approximately 90–110 minutes
2. 4–6 cycles per night
3. REM periods increase from 10 to 60 minutes.

D. REM/NREM Sleep

1. **REM**—Rapid Eye Movement Sleep
   a. Discovered in part by the research of E. Aserinsky and N. Kleitman (1953)
   b. Charles Dement 1954—Stages of sleep
   c. Transitional 5-10 plus duration, slowed heart rate and breathing, lightest level of sleep
   d. Sleep spindles, etc.
   e. EEG patterns

2. **NREM**—Non Rapid Eye Movement Sleep
   a. Delta increase from stage 2-4
   b. Delta EEG 20% Stage 2, 20-50% Stage 3, 50% plus Stage 4

	REM	NREM
EEG	Beta	Delta
EOG	Burst Eye Activity	Slow Drift
EMG	Tonic Immobility	Normal Muscle Ten.
HR	Rapid	Slow
Resp.	Rapid IRR	Slow Reg.
Dreams	Imagery Bound	Cognitive

E. Sleep Deprivation

1. Delirium
2. Hallucinations
3. Delusions
4. REM and NREM sleep deprivation and rebound effects

F. Sleep Disorders

1. Insomnia
2. Sleepwalking (sonambulism)
3. Narcolepsy
4. Sleep Apnea
5. Sleep Paralysis
6. Night Terrors

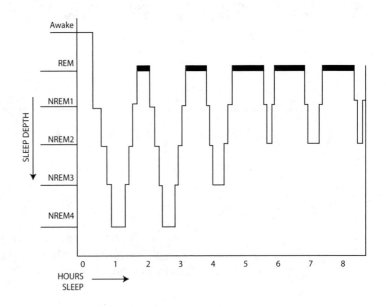

II. Theories of the Functions of Dreams

A. Tension-reduction Theory

Reduces tensions that are accumulated during the day

B. Freud's Theory of Dream Function

1. Dreams prevent a person from awakening.
2. Wish-fulfillment theory—Dreams attempt to fulfill our wishes (often unconscious).

C. Jung's Theory of Dream Function

Compensatory theory—person compensates in his dreams for what is lacking in his waking life

D. Problem Solving Theory

Dreams serve the same function as thinking. Dreaming is a continuation of the problems experienced during the day and an attempt to deal with them (e.g., Cartright).

E. Dreams as Brain Activity

1. Hobson and McCarley
Activation-synthesis hypothesis
REM sleep is a result of spontaneous, periodic activity of the brain stem (pons), producing random cortical activity. The cortex then acts to synthesize these essentially random images by forming a dream from memory images. The dream is therefore a byproduct of periodic brain activation rather than as a result of unconscious wishes (i.e., Freud).

F. Evolutionary Memory Function

III. Symbolism

A. A Symbol Is Something that Stands for Something Else.

B. A Referent Is the "Something Else" a Symbol Stands for.

C. Denotative Symbolism Refers Specifically and Literally to an Object or Event.

D. Metaphorical Symbolism Stands for Something Other than What It Appears to Be.

E. Freud's Theory of Symbolism

Disguise Theory—Symbols serve to conceal the true meaning of a dreamer's thoughts from himself.

F. Jung's Theory of Symbolism

"The symbol is not a sign that veils something everybody knows. Such is not its significance; on the contrary, it represents an attempt to elucidate, by means of analogy, something that still belongs entirely to the domain of the unknown or something that is yet to be."

IV. Techniques for Analyzing Symbols

A. Freud

1. **Manifest content** is the dream as dreamed and recalled.
2. **Latent content** is the thoughts and feelings about the manifest content.
3. **Free association** is used for interpretation.

B. Jung

1. Amplification
   a. A cluster of associations around a dream element
   b. Paint or sculpt significant dream images
   c. *Reflection* on "sand tray" reproductions of dream content

C. Dream Series Method and Content Analysis

1. **Dream Series Method**—A record of dreams is made until there is an accumulation of 50–100, then checked for recurring themes, preoccupations, etc., until a pattern emerges.
2. **Content Analysis**—Uses a set of categories which the dream elements can be placed into

D. Gestalt Approach

All dream content are viewed as constructions and projections of some aspect of the individual's personality. To elucidate the meaning of dream content Fritz Perls suggests that you give a "voice" to each of the important images in the dream.

V. Drugs

Drugs are chemical substances that have particularly strong influences on awareness, experience, and behavior. The study of such drugs is called *Psychopharmacology.*

A. Drugs and Addiction

1. **Addiction**
   a. Hypersensitivity theory—opponent process theory
   b. Psychological / physiological dependency
   c. Magnitude varies w/ amount of tolerance over time.
2. **Tolerance**
3. **Withdrawal**

B. Major Types of Abused Drugs

1. **Sedatives or Hypnotics**/Depressants
   a. Barbiturates—(eg. sleeping pills)
   b. Benzodiazepines (mild tranquilizers)
   c. Alcohol
   d. Major Tranquilizers (eg. Thorazine)
2. **Narcotics**/Analgesics
   a. Opium alkaloids
      1) Morphine
      2) Heroin (savior, "horse")
   b. Synthetic Analgesics
      1) Demerol
      2) Seconal
      3) Vicoden
      4) Oxycodon

3. **Stimulants:** Reduce appetite, fatigue, depression and the need for sleep
   a. **Amphetamines** (Amphetamine Sulfates)
      1) Dexedrine
      2) Benzedrine
      3) Methamphetamines (eg. speed, crank, ice, meth)
   b. **Cocaine**
      1) "crack"
   c. Caffeine
4. **Hallucinogens**
   a. Alter perception and awareness of time & space
      1) Distortions - Delusions
      2) Hallucinations
   b. PCP
   c. LSD
   d. Mescaline
   e. Psilocybin (eg. "shrooms")
   f. MDMA - Extacy
5. **Cannabis**
   1) Marijuana
   2) Hashish
   3) THC

VI. Hypnosis

Trance-like state of focused personal will, that, enhances awareness and relaxation.

A. Anton Mesmer

1. Animal Magnetism
2. Treatment of Psychoneurosis

B. Is hypnosis an altered state?

C. Most affective result is reduced willingness to report pain.

D. Physiological correlates?

Sensation

I. Major Concepts

A. Sensation

The stimulation of a sense organ by physical stimuli in the environment and the transduction of these physical stimuli into neural activity

B. Perception

Process by which the organism selects, organizes, and interprets sensations

C. Transduction

Is defined as the conversion of physical energy into neural activity. The process of transduction is described and illustrated below:

Each sense has its own set of specialized receptor mechanisms, each designed to respond to a specific form of physical energy. For example, for the auditory sense the physical stimulus is the mechanical wavelike movement of air molecules. This wavelike movement in turn produces an oscillating movement in a sequence of structures within the middle ear causing a corresponding wavelike movement to be transmitted to the fluid of the inner ear (cochlea) which results in the deflection or bending of the stereocilia which then produces neural activity in the auditory nerve.

In general all receptors transduce (change/convert) physical energy by changing the permeability of its membrane to sodium or potassium ions. This electrical change is called a *receptor potential*. This receptor potential is graded, i.e., that is, it tracks directly in an analog way changes in the stimulus. The receptor potential in turn produces a generator potential which is also graded. When the graded generator potential becomes strong enough (reaches threshold), it will produce an action potential in the axon of the sensory neuron.

D. Distal Stimulus

The actual size, shape, and color projected by the external physical object (e.g., a tree of a certain size, shape, and color)

E. Proximal Stimulus

The stimulus pattern produced on the receptor surface by the distal stimulus. For example, in the eye this corresponds to the retinal image produced by light reflected from an object (e.g., a tree) in the external environment. For example, due to the optics of the eye, the **proximal** stimulus projected on the retina is inverted or upside down (in fact the image of the tree is projected on the retina upside down and the brain turns it right-side up). In addition, the actual measured size and shape of the retinal image becomes larger and/or changes geometric shape as a function of distance and/or orientation of the object (**distal** stimulus).

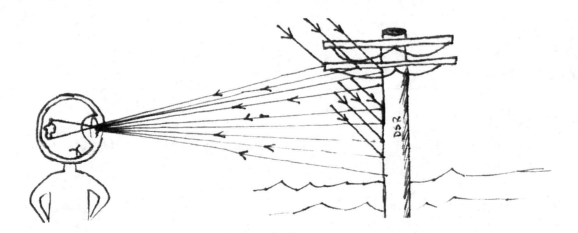

F. Psychophysics

The study of the relationship between the world of physical stimuli and the eternal world of sensation or sensory experience. Psychophysics also involves the measurement of the relationship between a physical stimulus and the psychological response to that stimulus.
1. **Absolute Threshold**—(also called *absolute limen*—Latin for "doorway") The minimum amount of stimulus energy needed to reliably produce a sensory experience 50% of the time (threshold is a statistical concept)
2. **Difference Threshold**—The minimum amount of stimulus change that can be detected 50% of the time. This difference is called a *just noticeable difference* or *jnd*. Historically the difference threshold was seen by Weber (1846) as a constant fraction of the stimulus, $??I/I = K–$. Fechner (1860) saw the jnd as growing arithmetically as the physical stimulus changed geometrically, $S = k \log I$. Finally, S. S. Stevens (1957) saw jnd as a power function rather than a log function, $S = k * I''$.

G. Theory of Signal Detection (TSD)

1. **Assumptions of TSD**
    a. Concept of central neural effect replaces concept of threshold in classical psychophysics. According to TSD all "signals" (stimuli) create some level of central neural effect whereby neurons are made to fire. It is assumed that both "signal" and "noise" condi-

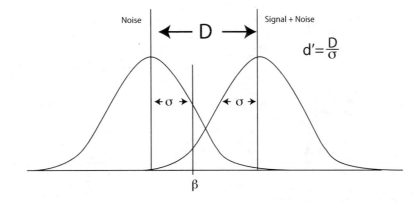

tions produce neural activity that varies from trial to trial in a normally distributed fashion. The "signal" and "noise" distribution curves always overlap. When the overlap is large (low signal to noise ratio), the subject's ability to discriminate between "signal" and "noise" is reduced.
    b. All "signals" are detected against a background of "noise." "Noise" is defined as any neuronal activity produced by internal and external events other than the "signal."
    c. The subject's willingness to report a "signal" is a function of the subject's decisional criteria.
    d. The subject's decisional criteria is a function of the subject's knowledge of (1) the payoff structure, and (2) the probability that the "signal" will be presented on a given trial.
    e. The payoff matrix
  2. **Concepts and Measures of TSD**
    a. Measures of the observer's sensitivity and/or signal to noise ratio (d^5) is calculated by measuring the distance between the means of the signal and noise distributions. The equation for calculating d'– is as follows: $d' = (Msn - Mn)/n$.
    b. Measures of the observer's criteria is called beta (B) which is calculated as follows: B = hit rate/false alarm rate.
    c. Receiver-operating characteristic curves (ROC)

H. The Visual System

  1. **Gross Anatomy of the Eye**
    a. Cornea—the transparent outer layer of the eye
    b. Iris—opening which controls amount of light entering eye (pupil)
    c. Lens—refracts (bends) and focuses light rays onto the retina
    d. Ciliary muscles—control the shape of the lens (accommodation)
    e. Retina—the first stage of visual information processing
  2. **Characteristics of the Visual Stimulus**
    a. Physical nature of light
      1) Photons
      2) Wavelengths and hue
        a) Visible spectrum (400–700 nanometers)
        b) Maximum response of RGB cones: blue green = 440nm, green = 540nm, red = 570nm
  3. **Structure of the Retina**
    a. Retinal blood supply (vascular layer)
    b. Neural layer (ganglion, bipolar, photoreceptor cells)
    c. Photoreceptors
      1) Rods—concentrated in the periphery of the retina, are most active for seeing in dim illumination, and do not produce sensations of color (about 120 million per eye)

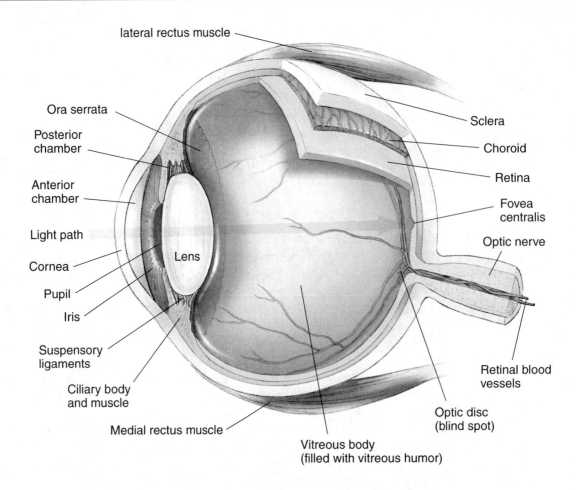

lateral rectus muscle

Ora serrata

Posterior chamber

Anterior chamber

Light path

Cornea

Lens

Pupil

Iris

Suspensory ligaments

Ciliary body and muscle

Medial rectus muscle

Sclera

Choroid

Retina

Fovea centralis

Optic nerve

Retinal blood vessels

Optic disc (blind spot)

Vitreous body (filled with vitreous humor)

2) Cones—concentrated in the center of the retina and responsible for visual experience under normal viewing conditions and for all experiences of color (about 6–8 million per eye); three types of wavelengths (Young-Helmholtz trichromatic theory)
- d. Fovea—area of the retina which contains densely packed cones and forms the point of sharpest vision
- e. Ganglion cells—axons become the optic nerve
- f. Bipolar cells—synapse between receptor cells and ganglion cells
- g. Horizontal cells—communicate across rods and cones; accounts for lateral inhibition
- h. Amacrine cells—communicate across ganglion cells; may participate in lateral inhibition cones, each tuned to respond maximally to either red, green, or blue
4. **Visual Pathways**
   - a. Optic nerve—one million fibers in each eye; produces the "blind spot" where it exits the eye
   - b. Optic chiasma
   - c. Lateral geniculate (LGN)
   - d. Superior colliculus
   - e. Visual cortex (Hubel and Wiesel: simple, complex, and hypercomplex cells)
5. **Theories of Color Vision**
   - a. Young-Helmholtz trichromatic theory (1850)
   - b. Hering's opponent-process theory
6. **Retinal Responses in Receptive Fields**
   - a. On off responses, center vs. surround comparisons
   - b. W cells are slowest; X cells for fine detail, quicker than W cells; Y cells for basic forms, fastest
7. **Lateral Inhibition**—Suppression of adjacent receptor cells

I. The Auditory System

1. **Gross Anatomy of the Ear**
   a. Outer ear—pinna, auditory canal
   b. Middle ear
      1) Tympanic membrane (eardrum)
      2) Middle ear ossicles (bones) stapes (stirrup)
   c. Inner ear
      1) Oval window
      2) Round window
      3) Cochlearduct
      4) Basilar membrane
      5) Organ of corti
2. **Transduction hair cells-inner ear.**
   a. Place theory
   b. Volley theory
   c. Frequency theory

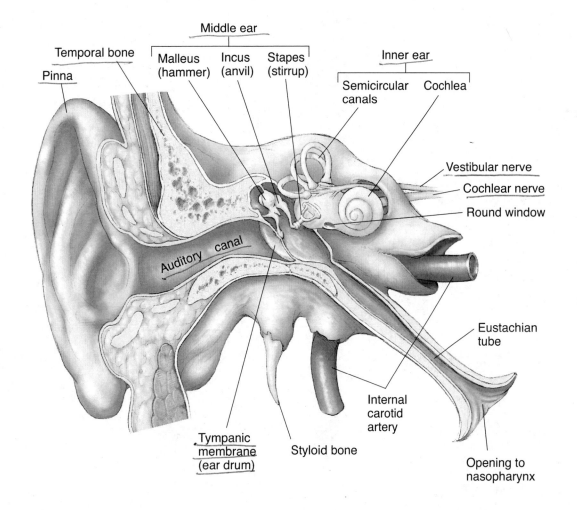

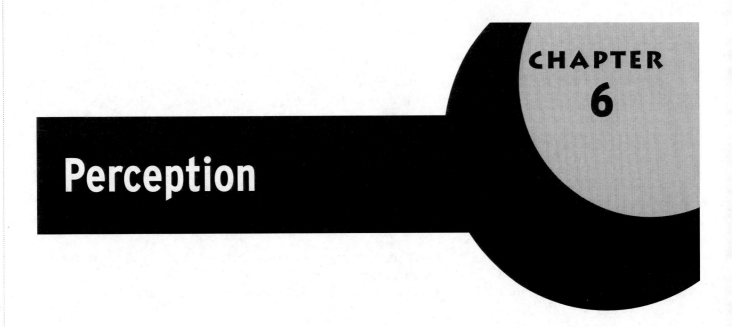

Perception

I. Perception Defined

While perception has been previously defined as the process by which the organism selects, organizes, and interprets sensations or sensory input, it is important to point out that perception as a process is viewed as a continuum from sense receptor response to cortical analysis and interpretation. It is not always clear where sensation ends and perception begins.

II. Theories of Perception

A. Nativism vs. Empiricism

1. **Nativism:** perception determined by innate internal mechanisms that interpret sensory stimuli
2. **Empiricism:** perceptual knowledge learned through experience and the environment

B. The Gestalt Approach

Emphasis on innate ways that the nervous system organizes stimuli into meaningful patterns or configurations. ("The whole is greater than the sum of its parts.") Early emphasis on a one-to-one correspondence between external stimuli and internal brain representations (isomorphism).

C. Constructive (Top-down Approaches)/Indirect

Rock, Neisser, Gregory all suggest that:
1. Perception is an active and constructive process.
2. Perception is not directly given by the stimulus input, but is the result of an interaction between the stimulus and internal hypotheses and expectations that serve as a basis for making inferences about the stimulus.
3. Since perception is influenced by internal hypotheses and expectations, errors may result.

D. Ecological (Bottom-up)/Direct

Gibson the major proponent of this theory suggests that visual perception is basically a bottom-up process wherein all the information needed for visual perception was potentially available from the proximal stimulus produced by the distal stimulus. Gibson's main theoretical assumptions are as follows:

1. The pattern of light reaching the eye can be thought of an optic **array** that contains all the visual information from the environment.
2. This **optic array** provides sufficient and accurate information about the layout of objects in space.
3. This information comes in the forms of **texture gradients, optic flow** patterns, and **affordances.**
4. Perception involves the **direct** apprehension of information provided by the optic array with little or no information processing involved.
5. Behavioral variability can occur as a result of differences in background experience given the same direct perception.

E. Theoretical Synthesis (Bottom-up and Top-down Processes Combined)

1. When a stimulus is presented long enough and clearly enough, perception may be largely bottom-up; however, as the duration is shortened and the clarity reduced, resulting in a more ambiguous stimulus, perception is more driven by a top-down processes.
2. In most circumstances perception combines the influences of bottom-up and top-down processes.
3. Neisser (1976) assumes that there is a perceptual cycle involving schemata perceptual exploration and the stimulus environment. Schemata are based on past experiences that serve to direct perceptual exploration toward environmental stimuli.

III. The Process of Perception

A. Selection

1. **Attention**
   a. Colin and Cherry—"Cocktail party phenomenon," dichotic listening
   b. Broadbent all-or-none filter theory
   c. Treisman attenuated filter model
   d. Late selection models

B. Organization and Perception

1. **Form Perception:** how sensory stimuli are organized
2. **Meaningful Shapes and Patterns**
   a. Pattern recognition theories
      1) Template theories—Stimulus information is compared directly to miniature copies, or templates, of stored patterns.
      2) Prototype theories—Pattern recognition involves the comparing of stimuli to prototypes, which are abstract forms representing the basic or most crucial elements of a set of stimuli (e.g., a prototypical airplane might consist of a long tube with two wings attached).

3) Feature theories—Pattern recognition begins with the *extraction* of features from the presented stimulus. This set of features is then *combined* and *compared* against information stored in memory (e.g., the alphabet may be decomposed into a set of twelve features—closed loops, horizontal line segments, vertical line segments, etc.).
4) Gestalt approach
3. Gestalt "Laws" of Organization Support PRÄGNÄNZ.
   a. Figure-Ground relationships
   b. Similarity
   c. Proximity
   d. Closure
   e. Good continuation
   f. Simplicity or figural goodness

C. Form Perception in the Brain

1. Hubel and Wiesel
   a. Simple cells—particular line location, place, and orientation
   b. Complex cells—receive input from simple cells and respond to lines of a particular orientation located anywhere in the visual field
   c. Hypercomplex cells—receive input from many complex cells and responds to particular shapes

D. Depth and Distance Perception

1. **Binocular Cues**
   a. Convergence
   b. Retinal disparity
2. **Monocular Cues**
   a. Accommodation
   b. Linear perspective
   c. Relative clearness or Aerial haze
   d. Interposition
   e. Shadows
   f. Gradient of texture
   g. Movement (Motion parallax)

E. Perceptual Constancies

1. **Size Constancy** (Emmert's law)
2. **Shape Constancy**
3. **Color Constancy** (Hue)
4. **Lightness or Brightness Constancy** (Mach bands and lateral inhibition)
5. **Orientation Constancy**

F. Movement Perception

1. Real Movement
2. Apparent Movement (phi phenomenon)
3. Induced Movement
4. Autokinetic Movement

G. Illusions

1. Ames Room
2. Ebbinghaus
3. Escher Drawings
4. Hering
5. Jastrow
6. Moon Illusion
7. Muller-Lyer
8. Necker Cube
9. Orbison
10. Poggendorf
11. Ponzo
12. Sander
13. Vertical/Horizontal
14. Zollner

Learning: Basic Processes

CHAPTER 7

I. Learning Defined

Learning is any relatively permanent change in behavior that is the result of practice or experience. Excluding changes due to fatigue, reflexes, drugs, instinctive or species specific behavior.

II. Basic Processes

A. Orienting Response

1. **Increased Sensitivity**
2. **Specific Skeletal Muscle Change**
3. **General Muscle Change**
4. **Brain Wave Change**
5. **Visceral Changes**

B. Conditions that Elicit Orientation

1. **Novel or Complex Stimuli**
2. **Conflicting Stimuli**
3. **Significant (Signal) Stimuli**
4. **Sokolov's Model—Habituation**
   a. Mild Stimulus
   b. Moderate Stimulus
   c. Intense Stimulus

C. Sensitization

Nervous System Supports Learning

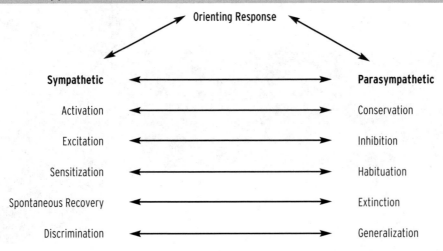

Orienting Response

Sympathetic		Parasympathetic
Activation	↔	Conservation
Excitation	↔	Inhibition
Sensitization	↔	Habituation
Spontaneous Recovery	↔	Extinction
Discrimination	↔	Generalization

Habituation–simplest form of learning defined as reduced response to repeated stimulation

Sensitization–increased response to repeated stimulation

Spontaneous Recovery–a return of the conditioned response after a rest period

Extinction–weakening of the conditioned response in the absence of UCS in classical conditioning, or reinforcement in operant conditioning

Discrimination–differing response to similar stimulation

Generalization–similar response to differing stimuli

D. Habituation and Sensory Adaptation

The organism ceases to respond physiologically and psychologically to a repeated stimulus that has no "new" information.

Eric Kandels Aplysia Studies

E. Dishabituation–return of the orienting response

III. Classical Conditioning–Pavlovian Conditioning

(Also called Respondent or Pavlovian conditioning) defined as an association or connection resulting from a repeated pairing of conditioned stimulus before presentation of the unconditioned stimulus Ivan Pavlov was a Russian Physiologist, one of his major discoveries was the conditioned response. Pavlov was interested in the function of the entire digestive process and used dogs as his research subjects. Dogs were ideal for a variety of reasons not the least of which was a prodigious and rapid salivary reflex. Pavlov won the Noble Prize for his work in 1904. The father of Russian physiology was M. Sechenov.

A. Key Terms

1. **Unconditioned Stimulus (UCS or US)**
2. **Unconditioned Response (UCR or UR)**
3. **Conditioned Stimulus (CS)**
4. **Conditioned Response (CR)**

B. Pairing Relationships of CS and UCS

1. **Forward Conditioning**—Generally CS overlaps onset of UCS
2. **Simultaneous**—simultaneous presentation of CS and UCS
3. **Delay**—CS is presented $\frac{1}{2}$ second before UCS and overlaps UCS.
4. **Trace**—CS precedes UCS by at least $\frac{1}{2}$ second and ceases before UCS.
5. **Backward**—presenting UCS before CS (What is learned?)
6. **Temporal**—Passage of time is the CS.
7. **Semantic**—conditioning by meaning

C. Requirements for Conditioning

1. Close temporal pairing (.5 second) between CS and UCS
2. A sense of contingency or predictability between CS and UCS (Tone becomes reliable predictor for presence of food/shock.)
3. UCS occurs independent of the subjects behavior. Ex: The subject does not perform an overt act or response.
4. Conditioned responses are usually associated with autonomic nervous system, primarily involving involuntary smooth muscle response (e.g., heart rate, GSR, pupillary response, vasoconstriction, visceral responses, etc. Exceptions: eye blink response and limb withdrawal to a painful stimulus).

D. Additional Principles and Applications

1. Extinction and Spontaneous Recovery
2. Stimulus Generalization
   a. Excitatory and inhibitory generalization gradients
3. Stimulus Discrimination
4. Sensory Preconditioning
5. Higher Order Conditioning
6. Blocking Effects (informativeness, redundancy)
   a. Overshadowing
7. External Internal Inhibition
8. Rescorla-Wagner Theory
9. Conditioned Emotional Response (CER)
10. Taste Aversion Learning—bait shyness
11. Applications to treatment of phobic reactions, anxiety, and sexual disorders

E. Treatment

1. Counterconditioning (general term)
2. Systematic Desensitization + Progressive Relaxation
3. Flooding/Implosive Therapy (virtual)
4. Aversive Conditioning
5. Negative and Positive Reinforcement

6. Cognitive Thought Stopping
7. Negative Practice
8. Cognitive Behavioral Therapy (CBT)

IV. Operant Conditioning / Instrumental Learning

A. A. E. L. Thorndike

1. **Connectionism**—Inferred unseen processes which mediated between stimuli and response
2. **Trial-and-error** learning as a gradual build-up of correct responses over reinforced trials (used cats as subjects in puzzlebox experiments)
3. **Mediating variables**
   a. Drives
   b. Response hierarchies
4. **Emitted behavior**
5. **Laws**
   a. Law of effect—Stimulus-response connections that are followed by a "satisfier" will be strengthened. An early version of the "law of effect" suggested that "punishers" would serve to weaken S-R connections. Thorndike's revised "law of effect" suggested that "punishers" do not weaken S-R connections, but may cause an indirect interference with learning through the effects of fear.
   b. Law of exercise—the repetition of rewarded stimulus-response connections
      1) Mere repetition by itself, in the absence of a reward or "satisfier," results in weakening the S-R connections (extinction).
      2) Repetition without knowledge of results (feedback) produces little or no improvement.

B. B. F. Skinner's Operant Learning (Conditioning "Penny" YouTube "Big Bang Theory" clip)

1. Skinner regards theories about internal states that go on inside the organism as neither necessary nor desirable. Rather, he believes it is more important to focus on relationships between observable behavior and its consequences.
2. Skinner's research emphasis was on studying response rates and response patterns. It was Skinner's view that behavior is shaped, maintained, and controlled by environmental stimuli. We are all determined by our reinforcement histories, rather than by internal, subjective goals, values, and purposes.
3. Positive reinforcement is "anything that increases the probability of the response."
4. Premack principle
5. Negative reinforcement is defined as the removal or avoidance of an aversive stimuli following an operant response. Therefore, responses that lead to the removal or avoidance of aversive stimuli are increased.
6. Escape and avoidance learning
7. Punishment is defined as response produced aversive stimuli, i.e., you make the response results in pain or discomfort. Therefore, responses preceding punishers will decrease because they lead to or cause aversive events.
   a. Characteristics of punishment
      1) Punishment suppresses responding, but does not necessarily eliminate behavior.
      2) The greater the punishment the greater the suppression of the behavior.
      3) Punishment is maximally effective when:

        a) Maximum intensity is used on the first trial. Gradual increases in intensity may lead to increasing adaptation or tolerance making punishment ineffective.

        b) It's immediate, consistent.

        c) Inescapable or certain, no reward possible

        d) Used in conjunction with positively reinforced alternative behaviors

    4) Negative aspects of punishment

        a) Conditioned emotional response of fear to stimuli associated with the situation (e.g., corporal punishment of children in school may lead to strong fear reactions to teacher and/or school in general, and if strong enough will lead to interference with the process of learning.

        b) Generation of counter-agression and hostility

            (1) Aggression can be directed at the object, e.g., teacher, school property, etc.

            (2) Aggression can be displaced.

            (3) Aggression can be turned inward.

8. In studying operant behavior, the first step is to record the level or frequency of the operant response (baseline) before the introduction of reinforcement. Ex: Before attempting to modify aggressive behavior of a group of school children by positive reinforcement methods, you must first measure the preexisting level of aggressive behavior.

9. Ways of eliciting the desired or terminal response (e.g., pressing a bar or pecking a key for food):

    a. Trial and error

    b. Forcing

    c. Providing a model

    d. Giving instructions (humans)

    e. Shaping or successive approximation

10. Discriminative stimuli

11. Preparedness—organisms come prepared to respond in species specific ways, e.g., pigeon pecking behavior, raccoon "washing" behavior, etc.

12. Response selection vs. teaching new responses

Summary of Schedules of Reinforcement

Type of Schedule	When Reinforcers Are Delivered	Effect on Rate and Pattern of Behavior
Ratio: Fixed (FR)	After a fixed number of bar presses	High rate of behavior with a pause after each reinforcer (partial reinforcement effect (PRE), post-reinforcement pause (PRP).
Variable (VR)	After a variable number of bar presses	High and steady rates of behavior (no PRP). Resistance to extinction high
Interval Fixed (FI)	For first response after a fixed amount of time has elapsed	Low rates of behavior at the beginning of the interval and high rates toward the end marked PRP (scalloped curve)
Variable (VI)	For first response after a variable amount of time has elapsed	Slow and steady rates of behavior (no PRP)
Concurrent	Two responses are involved (levers, keys). The relative **rate of responding to** each alternative matches the relative **rate of reinforcement** on each alternative.	In general, organisms prefer **immediate, small** reinforcement over **delayed,** large reinforcement. However, if an early commitment is involved, organisms tend to choose **larger, delayed** reinforcers.

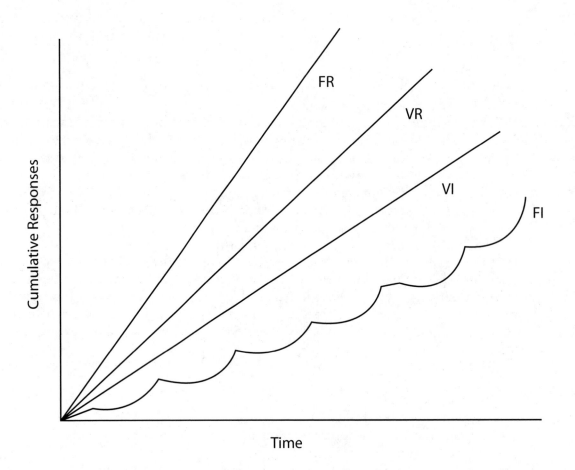

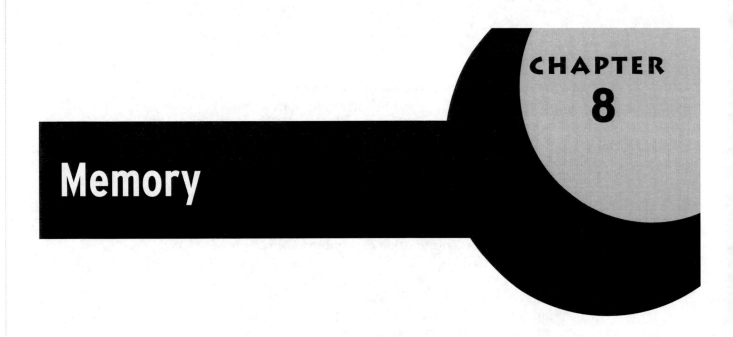

CHAPTER 8

Memory

I. Early Studies of Memory

A. Ebbinghaus Studies of Forgetting (1885)

1. The Nonsense Syllable—Trigram consonant—Vowel Consonant (e.g. TAV)
2. Curve of Forgetting

B. Measures of Memory

1. Recall
2. Recognition
3. Relearning (saving method)
4. Reintegration—Reliving memory

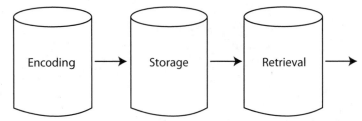

C. Theories of Forgetting

1. Memory Trace Decay
2. Motivated Forgetting
3. Interference Effects
   a. Retroactive and proactive inhibition
   b. Effect of activity vs. sleep on retention
4. Forgetting as a Failure in Retrieval (e.g., TOT)
5. Is memory permanent?

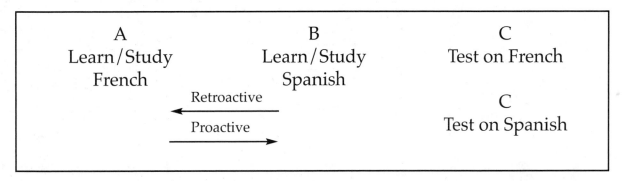

A Learn/Study French	B Learn/Study Spanish	C Test on French
	← Retroactive	C
	Proactive →	Test on Spanish

D. Memory Systems

1. **Sensory Memory** (Iconic, echoic, and tactile storage)
   a. Sperling's studies of Iconic storage—whole vs. partial report
   b. Averbach and Coriell's studies of backward masking
   c. Iconic storage—capacity, duration, decay effects
2. **Short Term Memory (STM)**
   a. Serial position effect
   b. Working memory—three subcomponents (Baddeley)
   c. Size, duration, and coding mechanism, chunking effects
   d. Maintenance rehearsal and elaborative rehearsal compared
   e. Sternberg's studies of short term memory retrieval processes
3. **Long Term Memory (LTM)**
   a. Encoding, size, and duration
   b. Mnemonics, method of loci, peg word, visual imagery
   c. Encoding specificity principle and state dependent memory
   d. Declarative and nondeclarative memory
   e. Semantic and episodic memories (Tulving), procedural
   f. Prospective and retrospective memory
   g. Dual-code hypothesis (Paivio)
   h. Levels of processing approach (Craik and Lockhart)
   i. Self-reference effect and state dependent memory
   j. Flashbulb memories
4. **Parallel Distributed Processing PDP** (Rumelhart)
5. **Neurobiology of Memory**
   a. Brain structures and memory
      1) Cerebellum
      2) Hippocampus
      3) Basal ganglia
      4) Limbic system

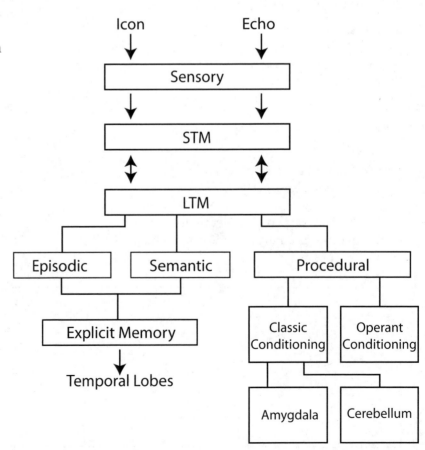

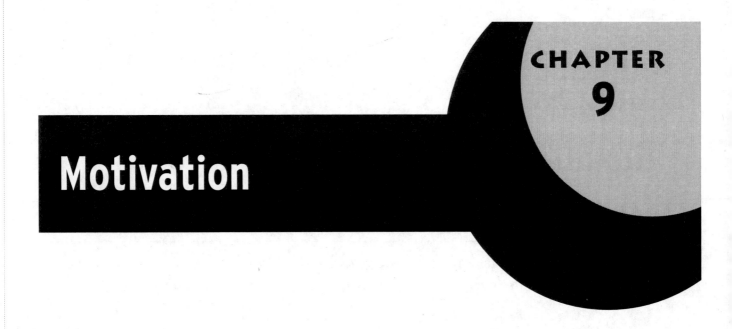

CHAPTER 9

Motivation

Motivation

An internal factor that arouses, directs, and integrates a person's behavior, not observed directly, but inferred from behavior

I. Theories of Human Motivation

A. Hedonistic Theories (Ancient Origin Maximize Pleasure)

B. Theory of Unconscious Motivation (Freud, Jung, etc.)

C. Instinct Theories (McDougall, Freud, Lorenz, and Tinbergen)

1. **Ethology** and instinct as fixed-action patterns released by environmental stimuli
2. **Evolutionary Psychology-"Sociobiology"**—Human social motives have genetic and evolutionary bases. Natural selection (Darwin) favors social behaviors that maximize the passage of genes to the next generation. Social motives such as competition, dominance, aggression, territoriality, and altruism are viewed in terms of their evolutionary purpose and value.

D. Humanistic-existential Theories (Maslow, Rogers, May)

E. Drive Theory—Behavioral Model

The concept of drive can be defined as an internal state of tension resulting from tissue needs (e.g., hunger, thirst) that motivates the organism toward activities that will reduce this aversive level of arousal. This process is called drive reduction and is used as a major motivational construct by behavior theorists such as Hull, Self-efficacy. (Bandura)

F. Arousal Theory

G. Opponent-process Theory

H. Incentive Theory

II. Physiological or Primary Drives

Basic idea is that an organic need exists (e.g., food, oxygen, water, etc.)

  Homeostasis—the overall term for all the equilibrium preserving tendencies

A. Hunger

  1. **Oral Factors**—Maintain eating behavior
  2. **Gastric Factors** (stomach contractions etc.)—Terminate eating via stretched receptor stimulation
  3. **Blood Chemistry** (blood sugar and fatty acid levels)—Start and stop eating
  4. **Brain/Neurological Factors**—Lateral hypothalamus = hunger – stops eating
      a. **Ventromedial Hypothalamus** = (VMH) satiation center – starts eating
  5. **Obesity**
      a. Fat cells
      b. Set point
      c. Stress

III. Human or Social Motives—Secondary Drives

A. Achievement Motivation—Conflict—Approach—Avoidance

B. Affiliation—Need to Be with Others—Gregariousness

C. Approval and Affectional Motives or Needs (Normal and Neurotic)

D. Abraham Maslow's Hierarchy of Needs

Self-Actualization
(becoming everything that one is capable of becoming)
Esteem
(including self-respect and feelings of success)
Belongingness and Love
Safety
(security, order, and stability)
Physiological
(satisfaction of hunger, thirst, and sex)

Human Sexual Behavior

I. Studies of Sexual Behavior

A. Freud's Psychoanalytic Perspective and Influence

B. The Kinsey Reports

Alfred Kinsey's conducted survey research of 5,300 American males in 1948 and published a study on male sexuality. In 1953, he conducted survey research on 5,940 American females and published a second volume on female sexuality. Subjects self-reported on their sexual behaviors including:
1. Masturbation
2. Nocturnal emissions
3. Petting to climax
4. Premarital intercourse
5. Marital intercourse
6. Extramarital intercourse
7. Intercourse with prostitutes
8. Homosexual contacts
9. Animal contacts

C. Kinsey's Data on Male and Female Sexual Behavior

1. Frequency—for all ages men an average 1–4 orgasms per week (range = 0–29). Changes in outlet frequency are related to age, social class, and religion.
2. Types of sexual expression, e.g., positions, forms of stimulation, etc., also vary with social class, religion, and educational level.

D. Masters and Johnson's Studies of Physiological Pattern of Sexual Response (1966–1970) Data Was Experimental, Interviews, and Observations n=700)

1. **Basic Pattern of Sexual Response**
   a. Excitement phase
      1) Male: erection (tumescence)
      2) Female: clitoral tumescence and vaginal lubrication
   b. Plateau phase
      1) Male: Testes increase by about 50 percent and are drawn up into the scrotum.
      2) Female: Tissues surrounding the vagina swell, the clitoris retracts under the hood that covers it.
   c. Orgasmic phase
      1) Male: Penis throbs rhythmically and semen is ejaculated.
      2) Female: clitoral withdraw, rhythmic muscle contractions and the orgasmic platform
      3) Both: Heart beats faster, blood pressure is elevated, and respiration is increased.
   d. Resolution phase
      1) Male: organs and tissues return to unstimulated condition (detumescence), and refractory period
      2) Female: slower resolution and capacity for restimulation and multiple orgasms
2. Frequency for women to experience multiple orgasms (14%)
3. Limitations of Kinsey's research
   a. Problems of self-report data
   b. Subjects were not representative.
   c. SES and education status shows frequency bias.

E. Sexual and Gender Identity Disorders

1. **Sexual Dysfunctions**
   a. Sexual Aversion
   b. Male Erectile
   c. Premature Ejaculation, etc.
2. **Paraphilias**
   a. Exhibitionism
   b. Fetishism
   c. Pedophilia, etc.
1. **Gender Identity Disorders (DSM-S Gender Dysphoria)**
   a. Transsexualism
   b. Gender Incongruence

Emotions

CHAPTER
11

I. Emotion–Adaptive Function

A. The Nature of Bodily Changes–Physiological Changes

1. **Activity of the Striped Muscles of Movement**
   a. Muscle tension
   b. Tremors
   c. Eye blinking and other nervous movements
   d. Vocal expressions
   e. Facial expressions
2. **Changes Controlled by the Autonomic Nervous System**
   a. Galvanic skin response
   b. Blood distribution
   c. Heart rate
   d. Respiration
   e. Pupillary response
   f. Salivary secretion
   g. Pilomotor response
   h. Gastrointestinal motility
   i. Blood pressure
   j. Blood composition

B. Emotion–Stress–Psychogenic Illness

1. **External Expression**
2. **Self Knowledge Function**
3. **Adrenal Medulla** (epinephrine and norepinephrine)
4. **Adrenal Cortex** (adrenalcortical steroids)

II. Theories of Emotion—Labeling

A. James-Lange Theory

B. The Cannon-Bard Theory

C. Cognitive Theories

1. **Cognitive Appraisal** (Lazraus)
2. **Two Factor Theory** (Schacter)

D. Facial Expression and Emotion (Eckman)

E. Plutchik's Wheel of Emotion

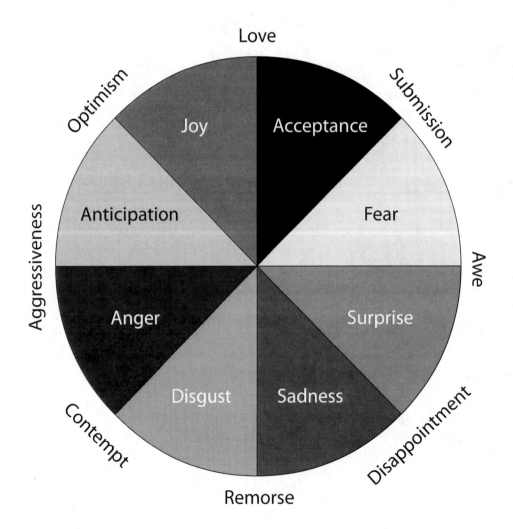

CHAPTER 12

Stress

I. Adjustive Demands and Stress

A. Categories of Stressors

1. **Frustrations**
   a. Lead to self-devaluation
   b. External and internal sources
2. **Conflicts**
   a. Approach-avoidance conflicts
   b. Double-approach conflicts
   c. Double-avoidance conflicts
3. **Pressures**
   a. Intensify efforts
   b. Internal and external sources
      1) High pressure careers
      2) Inner motivations
4. **Change**
   a. New context and conditioning
   b. Habit pattern conflict/pressure of new learning

B. Factors Influencing the Severity of Stress

1. **The Nature of the Stressor**
   a. Importance or significance of event
   b. Duration of stressor
   c. Number of stressors
2. **The Individual's Stress Tolerance and Resources**
   a. Perception of threat
      1) Uncertainty and inadequacy add to threat
      2) Less control promotes threat perception
   b. Stress tolerance
      1) Individual differences in ability to tolerate frustration

C. Individual Stressor Patterns over Time

II. Reactions to Life Stress (Chaos and Unpredictability)

A. General Principles of Reactions to Stress

1. **Task-oriented Responding**
   a. Changes may be required in self or environment.
   b. Provides for flexibility
2. **Defense Oriented**
   a. Protecting oneself from harm
   b. Stressor situation is unresolved.

B. Defense-oriented Reaction Patterns

C. Decompensation under Excessive Stress—Psychogenic Illness

1. **Effects of Severe Stress**
   a. Lowering of adaptive efficiency
      1) Proneness to disease increases
      2) Narrowing of perceptual field
      3) Impaired or disorganized performance
   b. Lowering of resistance to other stressors
      1) Series of stressors can reduce resistance to disease
      2) Stress and cancer development
2. **Biological Decompensation**
   a. Selye's general adaption syndrome (GAS)
   b. Permanent lowering of previous functioning level
3. **Psychological-decompensation**
   a. Alarm and mobilization
   b. Stage of resistance
   c. Stage of exhaustion
4. **Personality Types A/B—Type C?**
5. **Optimism v.s. Pessimism (M. Seligman)**
   a. Explanatory Style
      1) Origins
      2) Impact on Health

Personality

I. Personality Theories

A. Psychodynamic Theories

Emphasizes the unconscious, inborn motives or instincts

1. **Sigmund Freud**
   a. ID
      1) Reservoir of psychic energy, conservation, and displacement of energy and object-cathexis
      2) Basic drives and instincts in the ID
         Eros and Thanatos—life and death instincts
         Characteristics of instincts
         a) Source
         b) Aim
         c) Object
         d) Impetus
         e) Repetition compulsion
      3) Not directly available to the conscious
      4) Primary process thinking—fantasy and reflex
   b. EGO
      1) The EGO comes into existence because the ID cannot satisfy the organism's needs through appropriate, rational behavior. The EGO must match the ID's fantasy image with physical reality by secondary process using identification.
      2) Operates by the reality principle and self-preservation. Secondary process.
      3) The EGO is the executive of the personality.
      4) Anticathexes of the EGO restrain the ID forces.
   c. SUPEREGO
      1) Contains morals and ethics
      2) The conscience—guilt feelings—internalize NO
      3) EGO ideal—internalized positive values

FREUD'S STRUCTURE OF PERSONALITY

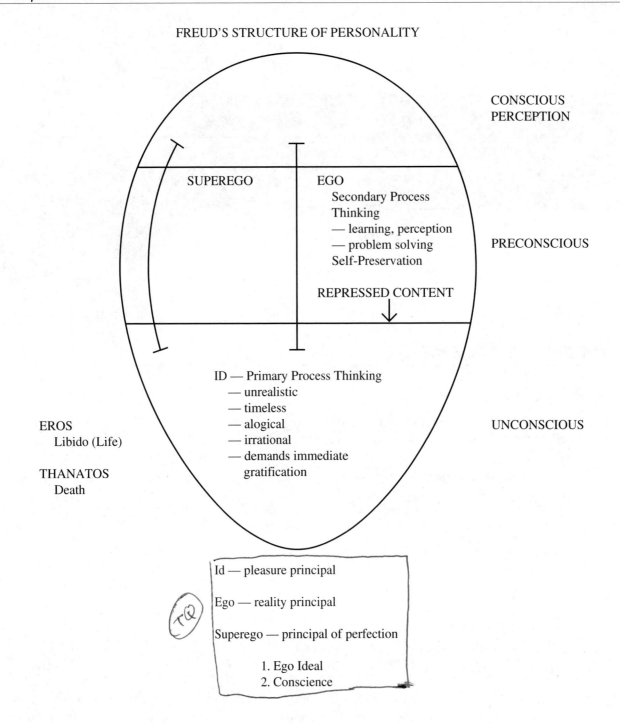

CONSCIOUS
PERCEPTION

SUPEREGO   EGO
            Secondary Process
            Thinking
            — learning, perception
            — problem solving
            Self-Preservation

PRECONSCIOUS

REPRESSED CONTENT

ID — Primary Process Thinking
    — unrealistic
    — timeless
    — alogical
    — irrational
    — demands immediate
      gratification

EROS
  Libido (Life)

THANATOS
  Death

UNCONSCIOUS

Id — pleasure principal

Ego — reality principal

Superego — principal of perfection

    1. Ego Ideal
    2. Conscience

Defensive Mechanisms

Compensation	Covering up weakness by emphasizing desirable traits or making up for frustration in one area by gratification in another
Denial of reality	Protecting self from unpleasant reality by refusal to perceive it
Displacement	Discharging pent-up feelings, usually of hostility, on objects less dangerous than those which initially aroused the emotion
Emotional insulation	Withdrawing into passivity to protect self from being emotionally hurt
Fantasy	Gratifying frustrated desires in imaginary achievements ("Daydreaming" is a common form.)
Identification	Increasing feelings of worth by identifying self with another person or institution, often of illustrious standing
Introjection	Incorporating external values and standards into ego structure so individual is not at the mercy of them as external threats
Isolation	Cutting off emotional charge from hurtful situations or separating incompatible attitudes into logic-tight compartments (holding conflicting attitudes which are never thought of simultaneously or in relation to each other); also called compartmentalization
Projection	Placing blame for one's difficulties upon others or attributing one's own "forbidden" desires to others
Rationalization	Attempting to prove that one's behavior is "rational" and justifiable and thus worthy of the approval of self and others
Reaction formation	Preventing dangerous desires from being expressed by endorsing opposing attitudes and types of behavior and using them as "barriers"
Regression	Retreating to earlier developmental level involving more childish responses and usually a lower level of aspiration
Repression	Pushing painful or dangerous thoughts out of consciousness, keeping them unconscious, this is considered to be the most basic of the defense mechanisms
Sublimation	Gratifying or working off frustrated sexual desires in substitutive nonsexual activities socially accepted by one's culture
Undoing	Atoning for, and thus counteracting unacceptable desires, or acts

Jungian Analytic Personality Structure

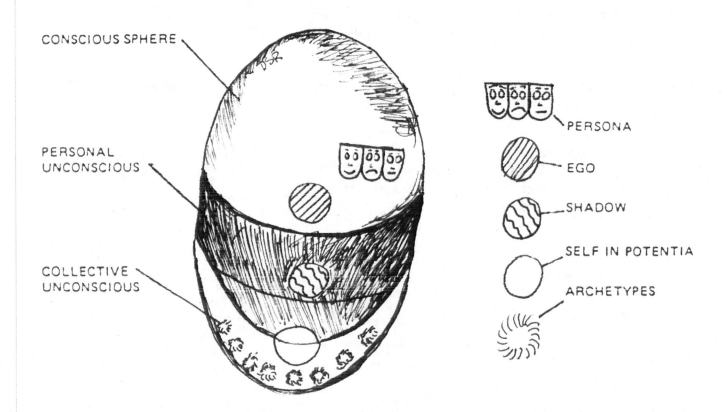

CONSCIOUS SPHERE

PERSONAL UNCONSCIOUS

COLLECTIVE UNCONSCIOUS

PERSONA

EGO

SHADOW

SELF IN POTENTIA

ARCHETYPES

2. **Carl Gustav Jung**—Analytical Psychology
   a. Rejected Freud's theories on
      1) Libidinal energy
      2) Determination of personality in childhood
      3) The inability of the adult to develop throughout life
   b. Levels of consciousness
      1) Conscious sphere
      2) Personal unconscious
      3) Collective unconscious
   c. Complexes and archetypes
      1) Persona
      2) Ego
      3) Shadow
      4) Self in Potentia
      5) Archetypes
   d. Psychological Types (Myers-Briggs Type Test)
      1) Attitudes
         a) Introversion
         b) Extroversion
      2) Functions
         a) Judgment and Evaluation
            (1) Thinking
            (2) Feeling
         b) Perception
            (1) Sensation
            (2) Intuition

B. Social Psychological Theories

1. **Alfred Adler**—Founder of Individual Psychology
   a. Teleological or future goal orientation (fictional goals)
   b. Inferiority feelings, compensation and overcompensation
   c. Striving for superiority
   d. Prototype—usually unconscious and consists, of lifeline and a goal directed strategy aimed at getting one's needs satisfied
   e. Style of life
   f. Birth order
   g. Social interest
2. **Harry S. Sullivan**—Interpersonal Theory
   a. Intra. vs. interpersonal structure and communication
   b. Levels of awareness
   c. Personifications
   d. Self-system (censor)
   e. Defense mechanisms—dissociation
3. **Karen Horney**
4. **Heinz Kohut/Melanie Klein**—Object Relations

C. Cognitive-Behavioral Theory

1. **Albert Bandura**—Cognitive Behavioral Model
   a. Reciprocal determinism
   b. Self system
      1) Self-regulation
      2) Self-observation
      3) Judgmental processes
      4) Self-reaction
2. **External Factors in Self-regulation**
   a. Standards of evaluation
   b. External reinforcement
   c. Selective activation
   d. Disengagement of internal control
      1) Redefinition of behavior
      2) Displacement of responsibility
      3) Disregard or distortion of consequences
      4) Blame the victim
      5) Disengagement and defense mechanisms
3. **Self-efficacy**
   a. Self-efficacy defined
   b. Sources of self-efficacy
   c. Self-efficacy as a predictor of behavior

D. Humanistic Personality Theory

1. **Carl Rogers**—Person-Centered Theory
   a. Basic assumptions
      1) Formative tendency
      2) Actualizing tendency
   b. The self
      1) Self-concept
      2) Ideal self
   c. Awareness
      1) Levels of awareness
      2) Denial of positive experiences
   d. Needs
      1) Maintenance
      2) Enhancement
      3) Positive regard
      4) Self-regard
   e. Conditions of worth

E. Biologically Based Personality Theories

1. Trait Theories
   a. Five Factor Model—R. McCrae and P. Costa 1987
   b. Extraversion-Intraversion—Psychoticism—H. Eysenck 1967
2. Type Theories
   a. Body Types—Ectomorph, Endomorph, Metomorph (M. Sheldon 1940s)
3. Evolutionary Models —D. Buss 1991

F. Existential Personality Theory—Philosophical Assumptions

1. Free will and self-determinism in choosing life goals, values, attitudes, purposes, and meanings
2. Emphasis on choice among alternatives—choice always exists in every situation with regard to actions, attitude, and meaning. Important life choices are always made under conditions of uncertainty and usually involve risk and pain.
3. Emphasis on responsibility for your choices—You are free to choose your behavior, attitude, or meaning, but you are totally responsible for this choice.
4. While you choose any behavior or value, you also choose the consequences.
5. Existential knowledge of our absolute separateness and aloneness in the world
6. The confrontation with and acceptance of death and the tragic aspects of life
7. The acceptance of our finitude leads to the affirmation of purpose and meaning in living (i.e., existential anxiety).
8. Authenticity—or being true to your own values and meaning, is a result of accepting full responsibility for what you are by recognizing that you can only be defined by someone else to the extent that you choose to accept this definition—you are totally responsible for your self-concept and life's meaning.

Assessment of Intelligence and Personality

CHAPTER 14

I. Requirements or Criteria for Test Construction

To qualify as scientifically sound a test should include the following:

A. Objectivity—Meaning that the Test Can Be Given and Scored in the Same Manner by Any Qualified Person and that the Results Will Be Unaffected by the Tester's Personal Opinions or Prejudices

B. Reliability—Yielding Similar Scores When the Same Person Is Tested on Different Occasions (e.g., test-retest, equivalent forms, split-half reliability)

C. Validity—Defined as the Ability of the Test to Measure the Characteristics that It Is Supposed to Measure. Some Types of Validity Are:

1. **Face or Content Validity**—direct, valid concepts of what is being tested
2. **Criterion or Predictive Validity**—test ought to predict future behavior in future tests
3. **Construct Validity**—scale that measures some aspect of personality that is related to many other forms of behavior

D. Standardized

1. Pretested on a large and representative sample so that an individual's score can be interpreted by comparison with the scores of other people (i.e., develop norms)
2. Standardized procedures for administration and interpretation

E. Types of Tests

1. **Group Tests**—administered to many people at once; usually lower in reliability
2. **Individual Tests**—given to one person at a time by a trained examiner
3. **Achievement Test**—measures how well the subject has mastered some specific topic
4. **Aptitude Test**—measures a person's ability to learn a new skill
5. **Criterion or Mastery Based Test**—test that measures the subject's performance in absolute terms

II. Intelligence Tests

A. The Binet-Simon Test (1905)

Originally devised by the prominent French psychologist Alfred Binet to identify slow learners

B. The Stanford-Binet Test (1916, 1937, 1973, 1986)

1. Includes scales to determine the IQ of adults
2. Drawback—Only American-born, white children were sampled.

C. Mental Age and IQ

1. MA (Mental Age)/CA (Chronological Age) × 100 = IQ (Intelligence Quotient). Example: $10/8 = 1.25 \times 100 = 125$, which is the IQ.

D. Deviation IQ Based on Normative Samples from Each Age Group Replaced the Mental Age Formula.

E. The Wechsler Scales (1939, 1955, 1981)

1. **WAIS-R**—Wechsler Adult Scale (16 to 74 years)
2. **WISC-R**—Wechsler Intelligence Scale for Children (6 to 16 years)
3. **WPPSI**—Wechsler Preschool Primary Scale of Intelligence (4 to 6 1/2 years)
4. Distinguishing feature of this group of tests is that they yield three measures of intelligence: verbal, performance, and full scale IQ.

F. Group Tests

1. **Otis–Lennon Mental Ability Test**—series of five tests of varying difficulty, covering the school years from kindergarten to college freshman
2. **Armed Forces Qualification Test**—for prospective members
3. **Scholastic Aptitude Tests (SAT)**—intelligence tests standardized for high school seniors

G. Virtues of Intelligence Tests

All modern intelligence tests are objective and standardized and have a high degree of reliability.

H. Weaknesses of Intelligence Tests

1. The impossibility of devising a test of general or basic mental ability that is purely an aptitude test rather than an achievement test
2. They tend to favor people who have grown up in white middle class environments.

III. The Nature of Intelligence

Intelligence is the ability to profit from experience, to learn new information, and to adjust to new situations.

A. What Is Intelligence?

1. **Thurstone's Primary Mental Abilities**
   a. Seven primary mental abilities—verbal comprehension, word fluency, number, space, associative memory, perceptual speed, and general reasoning
   b. General factors
2. **J. P. Guilford** believes that intelligence is made up of as many as 120 different factors.
3. **Spearman's Factor Theory**
   a. General mental facility
   b. Specific mental capability
   c. Factor analysis
4. **Cattell's Fluid and Crystallized Intelligence**
5. **Hunt's Problem-solving Intelligence**
6. **Gardner's Eight Intelligences**
7. **Sternberg's Intelligence Triad**

B. IQ and Heredity

1. There is general agreement among scientists that heredity does influence IQ, but to what degree is a matter of debate.
2. Interaction between heredity and environment

C. IQ and Environment

1. Environment also plays a part in determining IQ.
   a. Social class
   b. Educational level of parents
   c. Stimulation, encouragement, motivation, and reward provided by parents
   d. Culture

D. Effects of Deprived Environments

The child from the deprived environment not only has less chance of developing the skills measured by the IQ test, but the longer the child remains in this environment, the lower the IQ score is likely to become.

E. A Last Word on the Heredity-environment Issue

1. Heredity probably sets a top and bottom limit on the individual's IQ score.
2. Environment determines where within this range the score will actually fall.

F. IQ and Age

1. Intelligence increases until age 20–30 and declines thereafter.
2. Fluid intelligence peaks at about 18–25 and crystallized intelligence continues to develop into middle age.

G. IQ and Occupation

H. The Mentally Retarded—IQ below 70

1. **Primary Retardation**—Genetic
2. **Secondary Retardation**—Trauma, disease
3. **Mental Retardation Caused by Biological Abnormalities**
   a. Down's syndrome
   b. Cretinism—caused by an abnormally low level of secretion by the thyroid gland
   c. Others caused by biological abnormalities in metabolism, malnutrition, injury to the brain at birth, and brain damage caused by diseases
4. **Classification Criteria**
   a. Borderline = IQ 68–83 average 10–12 years old
   b. Mild   = IQ 52–67 average 8–10 years old
   c. Moderate = IQ 36–51 average 4–7 years old
   d. Severe   = IQ 20–35 average 2–3 years old
   e. Profound = IQ 10 down average 1 ??

I. The Mentally Gifted—IQ over 130

IV. Other Kinds of Tests

Empirical scales measure a number of personality dimensions and consist of questions with fixed or structured answers. Theoretical scales measure single traits and are based on concepts of theories of personality.

A. Vocational Aptitude

1. **Strong–Campbell Interest Inventory (SCII)**—Empirical
   a. Interest patterns of known vocational groups
   b. Used for job counseling
2. **The Interest Test** (Vocational Guidance)

B. Personality Assessment—The following are some objective tests of personality.

1. **Minnesota Multiphasic Personality Inventory (MMPI)**—Empirically derived norms based on performance of populations of patients with known psychiatric traits
   a. Degrees of abnormality
   b. Used to categorize patients entering mental hospitals
2. **California Psychological Inventory (CPI)**—Empirical, questions similar to MMPI, but used to measure scales of normal personality

3. **Thematic Apperception Test (TAT)**
   a. Subject is asked to make up a story about each of 20 black and white pictures.
      1) What led up to the scene?
      2) What is happening at the moment?
      3) What the people are feeling and thinking
      4) The outcome of the story
   b. The psychologist interprets stories.
4. **Rorschach Inkblot Test**
   a. Ten cards with a symmetrical inkblot on each (Some are in color.)
   b. Person is asked what the inkblot reminds him of as the cards are presented to him one at a time.
   c. Response time for each is recorded and answers are scored using a very elaborate and complex system.
5. Other more informal types of projective techniques:
   a. Word association test
   b. Draw a person
   c. Draw a family
   d. Sentence completion test

Behavior Disorders

I. History and Criteria Relating to Behavior Disorders

A. Abnormal Behavior Has Been Variously Viewed through the Ages as Either Possession by Demons, Mental Illness, or a Result of the Problems in Living. Today, It Is Regarded as a Process that has a Rational Basis and Therefore Can Be Studied Scientifically.

B. Some Attempts to Define "Abnormal" Behavior

1. **Statistical Criteria**—behavior that occurs infrequently
2. **Consensual Criteria**—behavior that society generally perceives as dangerous, anxiety provoking, or socially disruptive—relative standards
3. **Subjective Distress**—fear, sadness, and loss of control
4. **Maladaptive or self-defeating behavior** that result in a loss of a sense of well-being and a fulfillment of potentialities
5. **Inability to love and work** (Freud)
6. **DSM-IV-TR** defines mental disorders as a clinically significant behavioral or psychological syndrome that is associated with distress, disability, or increased risk of suffering, death, pain, or loss of freedom.

C. Classifying Mental Disorders According to DSM-IV-TR

Multiaxial System
1. **Axis I:** Clinical Syndromes
2. **Axis II:** Developmental Disorders and Personality Disorders
3. **Axis III:** Physical Disorders and Conditions
4. **Axis IV:** Severity of Psychosocial Stressors
5. **Axis V:** Global Assessment of Functioning (GAF)

D. DSM IV—Organizational Structure

II. Anxiety-based Disorders (Neuroses)

A. Anxiety Disorders

1. Panic Disorder and Agoraphobia
2. Social Phobia
3. Simple Phobia
4. Obsessive-compulsive Disorder
5. Post-traumatic Stress Disorder
6. Generalized Anxiety Disorder

B. Somatoform Disorders

1. Somatization Disorder
2. Hypochondriasis
3. Somatoform Pain Disorder
4. Conversion Disorder

C. Dissociative Disorders

1. Psychogenic Amnesia and Fugue
2. Dissociative Identity Disorder
3. Depersonalization Disorder

III. Personality Disorders

A. Personality Disorders

1. Clinical Features of Personality Disorders
2. Types of Personality Disorders
   a. Cluster A
      1) Paranoid
      2) Schizoid
      3) Schizotypal
   b. Cluster B
      1) Antisocial
      2) Borderline
      3) Histrionic
      4) Narcissistic
   c. Cluster C
      1) Avoidant
      2) Dependent
      3) Obsessive-compulsive
3. Causal Factors in Personality Disorders

IV. Mood Disorders and Suicide

A. Major Depressive Disorder

B. Seasonal Affective Disorder

C. Postpartum Depression

D. Dysthymic Disorder

E. Bipolar Disorder

F. Manic Episode

G. Cyclothymic Disorder

H. Suicide
1. Clinical Picture and Causal Pattern
2. Suicidal Ambivalence
3. Suicide Prevention

V. Schizophrenia and Other Psychotic Disorders

A. Schizophrenia
1. Clinical Picture in Schizophrenia
2. Problems in Defining Schizophrenic Behavior
3. Subtypes of Schizophrenia
   a. Undifferentiated
   b. Paranoid
   c. Catatonic
   d. Disorganized
   e. Residual
   f. Type I versus Type II Schizophrenia
4. Biological Factors in Schizophrenia
5. Psychosocial Factors in Schizophrenia
6. General Sociocultural Factors in Schizophrenia

B. Other Psychotic Disorders
1. Brief Psychotic Disorder

   2. **Schizophreniform Disorder**
   3. **Delusional Disorder**
      a. Clinical picture in delusional disorder
      b. Causal factors in delusional disorder
   4. **Schizoaffective Disorder**

VI. Causal Factors in Abnormal Behavior

A. Perspectives in Causation

   1. **Primary, Predisposing, Precipitating, and Reinforcing Causes**
   2. **Feedback and Circularity ("vicious circles") in Abnormal Behavior**
   3. **Diathesis-Stress Model**

B. Biological Causal Factors

   1. **Genetic Endowment**
   2. **Constitutional Liabilities**
   3. **Brain Dysfunction**
   4. **Physical Deprivation or Disruption**

C. Psychosocial Causal Factors

   1. **Self-perception and Cognition**
   2. **The Self and Motivation**
   3. **Early Deprivation or Trauma**
   4. **Inadequate Parenting**

Basic Structure of DSM-5

   1. Neurodevelopmental Disorders
   2. Schizophrenia Spectrum and Other Psychotic Disorders
   3. Bipolar and Related Disorders
   4. Depressive Disorders
   5. Anxiety Disorders
   6. Obsessive-Compulsive and Related Disorders
   7. Trauma- and Stressor-Related Disorders
   8. Dissociative Disorders
   9. Somatic Symptom Disorders
   10. Feeding and Eating Disorders
   11. Elimination Disorders
   12. Sleep-Wake Disorders
   13. Sexual Dysfunctions
   14. Gender Dysphoria
   15. Disruptive, Impulse Control, and Conduct Disorders
   16. Substance Use and Addictive Disorders
   17. Neurocognitive Disorders
   18. Personality Disorders
   19. Paraphilic Disorders
   20. Other Disorders

Psychotherapy

I. Types of Psychotherapy

A. Classical Psychoanalysis

B. Neo-Freudian Approaches

C. Client-centered Therapy

D. Behavior Therapies

E. Cognitive Therapy

F. Biomedical Therapies

II. Common Elements in All Psychotherapies

A. Relationship

1. **Patient** has a perceived need to change motivation and expectancy of getting help.
2. The **therapist** brings knowledge, training, empathy, and integrity.

B. Emotional Release

C. Cognitive Learning (All Therapists Convey Therapeutic Objectives and Explanation.)

D. Conditioning (All Forms of Therapy Have Some Elements of Conditioning.)

E. Identification (Modeling or "Social Learning")

F. Suggestion–Persuasion

G. Reality Testing–Rehearsal of Ways of Coping

III. General Characteristics of Therapeutic Relationships

A. Rapport

1. Define a conscious feeling of harmonious accord and mutual responsiveness
2. Is seen as the single most important therapeutic tool
3. Confidentiality

B. Transference–Countertransference

1. **Transference** is the patient's unconscious attachment to the therapist of feeling and attitudes that were originally related to important figures in early life.
2. **Countertransference** is the therapist's unconscious or conscious emotional reaction to the patient.

C. Resistance–All Clients Enter Therapy with a Resistance to Change and Self-knowledge.

IV. Psychoanalysis

A. Definition

"Through analysis of free associations and interpretation of dreams, emotions and behavior are traced to the influence of repressed instinctual drives and defenses against them in the unconscious." (APA Psychiatric Glossary, 6th edition)

B. Characteristics of Psychoanalytic Therapy

1. **The Therapeutic Relationship and Structure**
   a. Lying down
   b. The analyst's invisibility
   c. Evenly hovering attention
2. **Free Association**—the most basic agreement between analyst and patient
   a. Abreaction
   b. Catharsis
3. **Dream Analysis**
4. **Resistance**—blocks to free association—missed appointments, breaks off therapy
5. **Interpretation** of resistance, free associations, dreams and symptoms
6. **Transference and Countertransference**—The development and the resolution of the transference relationship is viewed as essential to successful treatment.
7. **"Working Through" or Re-education**—follows the development of insight and takes up most of the treatment time
8. The patient becomes his or her own analyst.

V. Modern Psychodynamic or Neo-Freudian Therapies

A. Greater Emphasis on Conscious vs. Unconscious Processes, i.e., more ego centered than ID centered

B. Direct Face-to-Face Client Therapist Interactions

C. Less Emphasis on Sexual and Aggressive Conflicts

D. Less Emphasis on Past and More Concern with Present Problems

VI. Client-centered (or Person-centered) Therapy

A. The Central Hypothesis: There Is an Innate Tendency to Develop and Realize One's Potentialities (Self-actualization) i.e., to Maintain or Enhance the Organism.

B. Significant Others Impose "Conditions of Worth" on the Acceptance and Love for the Child and These Become Part of His/Her Self-concept.

C. Incongruence Develops between the Orgasmic Experiences and Conscious Awareness (Self-concept). The Client Begins to Discriminate (Subceive) between Experiences Worthy of Regard from Significant Others and Those Not Worthy of His/Her Regard. S/He Begins to Avoid or Deny His/Her Orgasmic experiences.

D. Psychotherapy Involves the Intervention into the Incongruence that has Developed between his Experiencing Organism and His Self-concept.

E. The Therapist Facilitates Growth through Developing Three Attitudes:
1. The therapist must be **genuine and congruent**—be "transparently real."
2. **Empathy**—The therapist must be sensitive to the client's phenomenal experiences.
3. The therapist must be **unpossessively caring** or confirming and show "unconditional positive regard" toward the client.

F. The General Processes of Therapy
1. Generate an atmosphere of "unconditional positive regard"
2. The accurate reflection of feelings—The therapy becomes a "mirror of feeling."
3. Empathy—The therapist is able to understand the phenomenal world of the client.
4. Focus on the present here-and-now feelings
5. A totally non-directive, non-evaluative, non-judgmental attitude expressed by the therapist is essential.
6. Clarification of already expressed feelings
7. No interpretation, no advice giving, no comparisons, no prescriptions for how to solve the client's problems
8. The client determines the content, pace, and the depth of self-disclosure.

G. Stages of Therapy
1. **First Stage**—Communication is about externals, little about self or feelings.
2. **Second Stage**—Feelings are sometimes described but as unowned past objects external to self.
3. **Third Stage**—description of feelings which are not now present—usually unacceptable or bad

4. **Fourth Stage**—Feelings and personal meanings are freely described as present objects owned by the self. Intense feelings are still denied.
5. **Fifth Stage**—same as fourth stage except previously denied feelings brake into awareness—without total acceptance
6. **Sixth Stage**—same as fifth stage except feelings are now experienced with immediacy and acceptance
7. **Seventh Stage**—comfortable following process of experiencing all feelings with no incongruence

VII. Cognitive Behaviorial Therapy

A. General Principles

1. **Behavior therapy** can be defined as the modification of responses through the application of experimentally established principles of learning.
2. **Maladaptive behavior** is viewed as either deficient or excessive. Thus, therapy involves increasing the incidence of appropriate behavior and decreasing behavior that is inappropriate in frequency, duration, or place of occurrence.
3. **Maladaptive responses** may be covert as well as overt.
4. **Behavior disorders** are viewed primarily as the result of faulty learning.
5. **Treatment** is directed toward the removal of the inappropriate behavior (symptoms) and toward learning new, more effective patterns of behavior.
6. Emphasis in treatment is placed particularly on the social environment as a source of stimuli that support symptoms but that can also support changes in behavior.
7. **RET**—A.Ellis
8. **Reciprical Determinism**—A. Bandura

B. Types of Behavior Therapy

1. **Systematic Desensitization**
   a. This technique was developed by Joseph Wolpe as a means of associating anxiety-eliciting stimuli with relaxation.
   b. Since anxiety and relaxation are incompatible reactions, the increase in the strength of relaxation responses will inhibit the anxious responses to the same stimuli.
2. **In Vivo Desensitization**—Subjects are treated by exposing the patient directly to anxiety-provoking situations, rather than to imagined scenes.
3. **Implosion Therapy and Flooding** (Stampfl)
   a. The subject is flooded with anxiety-eliciting sensations using two techniques:
      1) The therapist creates imaginary fear-evoking scenes.
      2) In vivo flooding with the therapist adding fresh anxiety-provoking cues as the client reports less anxiety.
      3) Virtual Reality Exposure
4. **Aversion Therapy**
   a. This therapy is based on straightforward classical (Pavlovian) conditioning procedures. Stimuli are associated with some strong, unacceptable responses such as nausea, pain, or extreme disgust.
   b. The noxious stimuli that are used to produce the response of aversion may be chemical, electrical, or visual (including virtual).
   c. Aversion therapy has most often been used in the treatment of habitual excesses (e.g., overuse of alcohol) and compulsive unacceptable or criminal social behavior (e.g., shoplifting, exhibitionism).

d. Considerable controversy has been generated both about the effectiveness of aversion therapy and the social appropriateness of aversive control of socially deviant behavior.

5. **Behavior Modification and Contingency Management**
   a. Behavior modification is conducted by the application of operant conditioning principles to the management of behavior problems.
   b. The basic principle of behavior modification is the control of the reinforcing consequences of behavior. Reinforcing consequences range from primary reinforcers, such as food, to secondary reinforcers, such as approval.
   c. Behavior modification has been used for the following behavior problems: language training of autistic children, self-care training of intellectually challenged children and adults, and socialization of regressed psychotic patients.
   d. Token economies—Some chronic wards of psychiatric hospitals, some training schools and institutions for mentally challenged children and adults are managed according to operant conditioning principles.
   e. Operant principles, combining rehearsal and modeling with reinforcement, have been used to modify maladaptive behaviors and to train social skills.
   f. Self-regulation techniques, subjects learn to manage their own reinforcing consequences, e.g., weight regulation and smoking.
   g. Biofeedback techniques—self-regulation of physiological processes, e.g., muscle tension and EEG
   h. Extinction strategies

VIII. Social Learning Therapy

A. Imitation of Models

B. Participant and Symbolic Modeling

C. Social Skill Training and Behavior Rehearsal

IX. Cognitive Therapy

A. Definition: Many Behavior Therapists Assume that Self-statements, Beliefs, and Expectations Mediate much Maladaptive Behavior.

B. Types of Cognitive Therapy

1. **Albert Ellis's Rational-Emotive Therapy (RET)** assumes that patients are maladaptive because they act on irrational beliefs about themselves and others.
   a. The goal of therapy is to eliminate or reduce the "irrational consequences" of irrational belief systems, which in turn reduces anxiety and hostility.
   b. Through confrontation and active interpretation the patient is helped to restructure behavior by adopting more rational beliefs.

2. **Aaron Beck's Cognitive Therapy** assigns major importance to correcting the faulty thinking about oneself and about the rewarding opportunities in one's present or future environment.
   a. The approach focuses on helping the patient overcome faulty perceptions, distortions in self-concept, and false judgments about relationships in the world.
   b. The therapist may begin at a behavioral level of working toward reduction of abnormal symptoms, but the underlying distorted attitudes must also be identified and challenged.
   c. Active testing of assumptions through a variety of problem-orientation tasks leads to engaging in new activities based on cognitive modification.
3. **Donald Meichenbaum** developed his cognitive approach to behavior modification by treating cognitions as internal verbalizations and images that in distressed persons may interfere with performance.
   a. In treatment, patients learn to identify and then replace the self-statements and self-instructions that are maladaptive.
   b. Treatment is also directed toward providing means of desensitizing tension-producing conditions and producing more successful coping behavior through reinforcing self-comments and reassuring imagery.
   c. As in the other cognitive therapies, a cognitive restructuring is the desired outcome of treatment.

X. Group Therapies and Family/Marital Therapies

A. Gestalt Therapy

1. **Fritz Perls,** father of Gestalt therapy said "every organism tends toward wholeness or completion." Anything that disrupts this Gestalt is harmful to the organism and leads to "an unfinished situation which needs to be finished or made whole."
2. **Emphasis on Projection**
3. **Focus on the present** as the only reality. Nothing exists for all of us except for the "here and now."
4. **Retrospective character** is overly sentimental about the past or blames parents for everything. This is the most frequent unfinished situation.
5. **Prospective character.** Fantasies about what lies ahead are no more real than the memories of the past.
6. **Resentment** is seen as the worst kind of unfinished situation that we can carry with us. People who are resentful have reached an impasse.

B. Transactional Analysis

1. **Ego States**—parent, adult and child
2. Focus on transactions defined as responses between two persons' ego states.
3. There are two levels of transactions: social level, which is overt or manifest, and the psychological level, which is covert or latent.
4. **Games**—defined as a series of transactions at both the overt and covert level which result in "payoffs" with specific bad feelings for both game players, e.g., "Kick Me" and "Yes But," etc.

5. **Strokes**—All social interaction is based on the need for "strokes." Strokes may be direct, indirect, positive, or negative.
6. **Script**—develop through one's early interactions with parents having been supportive or attacking toward the client as a child. As a child, the client had at some point decided that s/he was either OK or not OK.

C. Family Systems Therapy

1. The family is viewed as an open system.
2. Individual symptoms are the result of tensions within the family system.
3. The family is seen as an open system made up of "interlocking triangles" that can either increase or decrease emotional intensity and distance among family members.
4. Whenever two people become too close or too distant, a third person can be introduced to restore equilibrium to the system.
5. The "identified patient" plays a tension-reducing role in the family system.
6. Family therapy focuses on communication patterns and "rules" in the dysfunctional family system.

XI. Biomedical Therapies

A. Psychosurgery and Electroconvulsive Therapy

B. Chemotherapy

1. **Antipsychotic Drugs**—Phenothiazines
   a. Chlorpromazine
   b. Fluphenazine
   c. Clozapine
   d. Haloperidol
2. **Antimanic Drugs**
   a. Lithium
   b. Depakote
3. **Antidepressant Drugs**
   a. Tricyclics
   b. MAO inhibitors
   c. SSRI—Prozac, Zoloft, Paxil, Lexapro, Celexa, Luvox
4. **Antianxiety Drugs**
   a. Barbiturates
   b. Propanediols
   c. Benzodiazepines (e.g., Valium, Xanax)
5. **Dual-Action Antidepressants/SNRIs**
   a. Busparinone (Buspar)
   b. Venlafaxine (Effexor)
   c. Duloxetine (Cymbalta)
   d. Mirtazapine
6. **Norepinephrine-Dopamine Reuptake Inhibitors (NDPI)**
   a. Welloutrin
   b. Zyban
7. NRIs, SARIs, NDRAs (see list of antidepressants online)